LOST
MESSAGES FROM THE ISLAND

Lost: Messages From the Island
ISBN: 9781848562622

Published by
Titan Books
A division of
Titan Publishing Group Ltd
144 Southwark St
London
SE1 0UP

First edition June 2009
10 9 8 7 6 5 4 3 2 1

Visit our website:
www.titanbooks.com

Acknowledgments:
Titan Books would like to thank Melissa Harling and all at ABC for their continuing help with this
project, Larry Fong for his photographs on P114-118, and Paul Terry for giving us his time and
Lost expertise to ensure this is the best possible tribute to a landmark television show.

To receive advance information, news, competitions, and exclusive Titan offers online, please
register as a member by clicking the "sign up" button on our website: www.titanbooks.com

Did you enjoy this book? We love to hear from our readers. Please email us at
readerfeedback@titanemail.com or write to us at Reader Feedback at the above address.

A CIP catalogue record for this title is available from the British Library.

Printed and bound in China by C&C Offset Printing Co., Ltd.

CONTENTS

To Our Lost Fans,

It's hard to believe that we are already nearing the end of the fifth season of the show, especially since almost no one thought we would make it past the first twelve episodes. The true credit for that goes to you, our fans! All of us here at Lost are deeply indebted to you for your devotion to our show.

And thank you for picking up this collection of Lost Magazine's best articles. There is a lot of cool show history and background information to be read in here, stories that nicely compliment viewing the episodes.

We are grateful to Lost Magazine for helping document the journey of our show. Many people deserve credit for that. We have to single out Paul Terry, Melissa Harling, Samantha Thomas, Gregg Nations and Noreen O'Toole for special praise. They have all put in count-less hours making the magazine be as good as it is.

We are equally blessed to have an amazing ensemble of talent who work on Lost. Our superlative writers and directors, our amazingly talented production and post-production teams in concert with the best damn cast on television come together to make what we hope you agree is something pretty darn special.

We hope you enjoy this engaging and entertaining slice of Lost history.

Peace, Love and Namaste,

WE ARE THE PASSE

Remind yourselves of the backgrounds of the survivors of Oceanic Flight 815,

Oceanic Airlines | **ECONOMY CLASS**

REQUIREMENTS / REMARKS/ IDENTIFICATION

Jack Shephard

Played by: Matthew Fox
Occupation: Surgeon

BACKGROUND:
The reluctant leader of the survivors, Jack traveled to Sydney in search of his missing and estranged father, only to discover him recently deceased. Jack was on flight 815 returning to LA with his father's body.

FROM:	TO:	FLIGHT:	BOARDING TIME:	SEAT No.
SYD	LAX	815	14:15	

Oceanic Airlines | **ECONOMY CLASS**

REQUIREMENTS / REMARKS/ IDENTIFICATION

Kate Austen

Played by: Evangeline Lilly
Occupation: Fugitive

BACKGROUND:
On the run from the law, Kate was caught by the Marshall in Australia and was being extradited to the US to stand trial.

FROM:	TO:	FLIGHT:	BOARDING TIME:	SEAT No.
SYD	LAX	815	14:15	

NGERS

both those at the front of the plane and those know as the 'Tailies'...

Oceanic Airlines — ECONOMY CLASS

REQUIREMENTS / REMARKS/ IDENTIFICATION

James 'Sawyer' Ford

Played by: Josh Holloway
Occupation: Con man

BACKGROUND:
Took on the persona of the man who destroyed his family, Sawyer is obsessed with hunting down the original 'Sawyer' and avenging his parents' deaths.

FROM:	TO:	FLIGHT:	BOARDING TIME:
S Y D	L A X	815	14:15

Oceanic Airlines — ECONOMY CLASS

REQUIREMENTS / REMARKS/ IDENTIFICATION

John Locke

Played by: Terry O'Quinn
Occupation: Collections manager at a box company.

BACKGROUND:
Once wheelchair bound, the survival expert was miraculously able to walk again after the crash. Locke was brought up in a foster home, as an adult he found his ailing biological father who conned a kidney out of him and then cruelly cut him off.

FROM:	TO:	FLIGHT:	BOARDING TIME:
S Y D	L A X	815	14:15

TAIL EXPLOSION

BREAKING POINT

MID SECTION EXPLOSION

ECONOMY CLASS

Oceanic Airlines

REQUIREMENTS / REMARKS/ IDENTIFICATION

Claire Littleton

Played by: Emilie de Ravin
Occupation: Mother

BACKGROUND:
Abandoned, pregnant, by her boyfriend, Claire visited a psychic who told her that only she should raise her child. Despite this she decides to give it up for adoption and boards a plane to LA to meet a suitable couple.

FROM: SYD TO: LAX FLIGHT: 815 BOARDING TIME: 14:15

ECONOMY CLASS

Oceanic Airlines

REQUIREMENTS / REMARKS/ IDENTIFICATION

Sayid Jarrah

Played by: Naveen Andrews
Occupation: Formerly a member of the Iraqi Republican Guard.

BACKGROUND:
Tortured and interrogated prisoners for the Iraqi government, Sayid sacrificed his career to save his childhood love Nadia. He was on his way to LA to be reunited with her.

FROM: SYD TO: LAX FLIGHT: 815 BOARDING TIME: 14:15

Oceanic Airlines

ECONOMY CLASS

REQUIREMENTS / REMARKS/ IDENTIFICATION

Charlie Pace

Played by: Dominic Monaghan
Occupation: Has-been rock star

BACKGROUND:
Once in a briefly popular band called Drive Shaft. Charlie was in Sydney to persuade his former heroin-addict brother to reform the band. His brother refused and tried to persuade Charlie to kick his own drug habit, but Charlie left and boarded flight 815 to LA.

FROM:	TO:	FLIGHT:	BOARDING TIME:
SYD	LAX	815	14:15

 Oceanic Airlines

ECONOMY CLASS

REQUIREMENTS / REMARKS/ IDENTIFICATION

Hugo 'Hurley' Reyes

Played by: Jorge Garcia
Occupation: Fast food employee turned lottery winner.

BACKGROUND:
$156 million lottery winner and former mental patient, Hurley's astonishing run of bad luck leads him to believe his winning lottery numbers were cursed. He almost missed the flight but made it on board despite many omens warning him to stay off the plane.

FROM:	TO:	FLIGHT:	BOARDING TIME:
SYD	LAX	815	14:15

ECONOMY CLASS

 Oceanic Airlines

REQUIREMENTS / REMARKS/ IDENTIFICATION

Michael Dawson

Played by: Harold Perrineau
Occupation: Construction

BACKGROUND:
Recently attained custody of his son, Walt, after his ex-wife's death and came to Sydney to collect him. He is stranded on the island with his son and his son's dog, Vincent.

FROM:	TO:	FLIGHT:	BOARDING TIME:
SYD	LAX	815	14:15

ECONOMY CLASS

Oceanic Airlines

REQUIREMENTS / REMARKS/ IDENTIFICATION

Jin-Soon Kwon

Played by: Daniel Dae Kim

BACKGROUND:
Once a loving husband to Sun, the couple became increasingly estranged as Jin was coerced into working for her unscrupulous father. Sent by him to Sydney and the US, Jin was planning to escape his violent job and remain in the US with Sun indefinitely.

FROM:	TO:	FLIGHT:	BOARDING TIME:	
SYD	LAX	815	14:15	

ECONOMY CLASS

Oceanic Airlines

REQUIREMENTS / REMARKS/ IDENTIFICATION

Sun-Soo Kwon

Played by: Yunjin Kim

BACKGROUND:
Daughter of a powerful auto magnate, she married Jin, a servant in her family. As her marriage fell apart, she secretly learned English and considered faking her own kidnapping in order to leave Jin. At the last minute she elected to board flight 815 and stay with her husband.

FROM:	TO:	FLIGHT:	BOARDING TIME:	
SYD	LAX	815	14:15	

ECONOMY CLASS

Oceanic Airlines

REQUIREMENTS / REMARKS/ IDENTIFICATION

Mr. Eko

Played by: Adewale Akinnouye-Agbaj

BACKGROUND:
Born and raised in Nigeria, Mr. Eko served as a priest in England and then Australia and is weighed down by guilt at having caused the death of his brother, Yemi. Having trained as a guerrilla fighter in Nigeria, he has an almost savage ability to fight and kill.

FROM:	TO:	FLIGHT:	BOARDING TIME:	
SYD	LAX	815	14:15	

Oceanic Airlines **ECONOMY CLASS**

REQUIREMENTS / REMARKS/ IDENTIFICATION

Ana Lucia Cortez

Played by: Michelle Rodriguez

BACKGROUND:
Once an officer in the Los Angeles Police Department, she was pregnant and lost her baby when a suspect shot her at a burglary scene. Later she tracked down the shooter and killed him. She came to Sydney acting as Christian Shephard's bodyguard.

FROM:	TO:	FLIGHT:	BOARDING TIME:
SYD	LAX	815	14:15

ECONOMY CLASS

Oceanic Airlines

REQUIREMENTS / REMARKS/ IDENTIFICATION

Libby

Played by: Cynthia Watros

BACKGROUND:
A clinical psychologist, Libby was once married to a man name David who gave her a sailboat named after her, *Elizabeth.* She is emotional and caring and tries to keep people as calm as possible.

FROM:	TO:	FLIGHT:	BOARDING TIME:
SYD	LAX	815	14:15

LEADERS OF THE PACK

The union began with Kate healing Jack's wound in the pilot episode. Since then, both characters have gotten under each other's skin. **MATTHEW FOX** and **EVANGELINE LILLY** discuss the pair's evolving relationship…

"There is no question that I love the challenge of playing this guy and I think he is amazing. He has an enormous amount on his plate and is doing everything he can to live up to his own expectations..."
— Matthew Fox

Amidst the flames and panic of the

crashed remains of Oceanic Flight 815 on *Lost*, there quickly emerged a duo that would evolve into the unofficial leaders of the initial 48 survivors: Jack (Matthew Fox), the upstanding and brave doctor that administered to the injured and those in peril from the moment he walked onto the wreckage strewn beach, and Kate (Evangeline Lilly), the guarded and calculating young woman that hand-stitched a nasty gash on Jack's back, immediately forging a bond between the two. Fate has a funny sense of humor though, and while Jack and Kate initially appeared to be kindred spirits of integrity and empathy, it soon became clear this was anything but the case. Sure, Jack was pretty much the all-American real deal, but Kate was a whole *other* story. A fugitive from justice with a wickedly deceptive past, the seeming good girl was far more of a bad girl. As the season progressed and more about Kate's past was unearthed, Jack was increasingly more disturbed to find out how dissimilar they were. Yet they retain a connection that crackles with chemistry.

For actors Matthew Fox and Evangeline Lilly, that strong connection – despite their obvious differences – applies to their real world lives too. Fox is a television veteran of shows like *Party of Five* and *Haunted*, while Lilly was an acting unknown when she first stepped onto the sands of Hawaii to shoot the *Lost* pilot. Fox is a married father with two children, while Lilly is single and still in her 20s. He's Wyoming born and bred, while she's Canadian. Yet for all their differences, Fox and Lilly have crafted an on-screen pairing that's been electric for audiences to watch and root for over the past year. You can't explain chemistry, but the pair were more than happy to spend some time with *Lost Magazine* to dissect their working relationship and talk about the highlights of their incredible, whirlwind first season on *Lost*.

Jumping into the lead role of Jack over a year ago, Fox says he was more than ready to take on the responsibilities of helping to carry this unique show. "I talked to J.J. [Abrams] and Damon [Lindelof] a lot about my responsibilities as number one on the call sheet," Fox explains. "In between *Party of Five* and this, I did a show called *Haunted* that I was very, very proud of and I was the single lead in that show. I think I earned my stripes a little bit to take on that kind of responsibility [with *Lost*] and I felt great about it. I was incredibly excited about the show. I love it and I really believe in it. It's demanding, physically and emotionally, to take on that responsibility, but as far as me wanting to do it, I really felt ready and willing."

Lilly laughs at her own distinct lack of experience when cast on the series. "I was most nervous that I was jumping in and I was way over my head – that I was out of my league and I was treading dangerously in unfamiliar waters that maybe I wasn't cut out to tread in," she admits candidly. "For me, it was a huge concern. I'm standing next to some actors that I have come to absolutely admire and respect. I'm being measured with the same stick as them because I'm on the same television program as they are – it's terrifying!"

Yet, Lilly says it was Fox who helped her settle into the show so quickly, by basically brushing her off. "Honestly, probably the biggest sigh of relief was when I first met Matthew. He seemed so uninterested in me, like absolutely unfazed that we were meeting," she laughs. "He was like, 'Oh, yeah, OK, hi,' and he just moved on with his conversation he was in the middle of. I just took that as a wonderful sign that he and I were going to be able to be on a really comfortable level with one another. There wasn't going to be any cheesy Hollywood fakeness or superficiality in our relationship. The second most encouraging thing when I met him was to find out he was happily married with two children, because I think when you are playing romantic leads in a television show together, you always run the risk that real emotions might get involved and come into play. Finding out he was happily married was so reassuring to me, because I was far from interested in having that very awkward dynamic come into play with my leading man."

ON THE FIRST DAY

EVANGELINE LILLY and **MATTHEW FOX** relive the moments the *Lost* cameras first rolled...

"My first day on the set was with Matthew Fox and Dominic Monaghan. We had an instant connection, the three of us, and became instant buddies. We had an amazing time filming the pilot together and are very close."
– Evangeline Lilly

"The first day I shot on the set was in the jungle and it was a really rough day. A lot of it was the post-cockpit sequence, when we are running from the 'thing' and I remember feeling very excited. It was mainly an action day and it was really muddy. We were soaking wet and cold and I was thinking to myself, 'This is going to be demanding,' but I was also very excited."
– Matthew Fox

With *Lost* literally evolving from episode to episode in the Writers' Room back in Los Angeles, all the actors were required to trust in their character evolution over the season, adjusting and refining as they went along. But for Fox, he says Jack was absolutely clear to him from day one. "Damon and I talked about Jack so much early on in general terms about who he is as a man and how he approaches the world and challenges. We talked about his convictions and his moral code. So much so, that Damon can take that story wherever he wants to. He can even fill in the back-story, but it's always going to fit in the realm of the man that we both subconsciously know. There is no question that I love the challenge of playing this guy and I think he is amazing. He has an enormous amount on his plate and is doing everything he can to live up to his own expectations within that. He sets the bar incredibly high for himself and doesn't like the idea of failure. I enjoy him and think that he's a really strong individual."

For Lilly, Kate has been far more challenging in that she started out as a seemingly wide-eyed innocent and ended up *far* from that paragon of virtue by season's end. "I think, initially, what really characterized how I felt about her was that I was very much in the dark," Lilly reflects. "I spent the pilot turning to J.J. constantly saying, 'So, how should I be playing this scene? I don't know her or where she is coming from or what she's done.' He initially did a lot of hands-on directing with me. As time went on throughout the season, we started filling in the puzzle pieces. I was more able to come to set with an idea in my mind of exactly how I thought Kate would react to a situation and not feel nearly as in the dark, which was a really nice place to come to. In some respects, you have more creative freedom as an actor, but it can also be frustrating because there is more chance I'm going to butt heads with the director if he happens to have a different idea of how the role or the situation should be played. I'm now coming in saying, 'I know Kate! I know her inside-out and this is how I think she would be.' Our Director/Producer Jack Bender, who I work with on a regular basis, he and I have a really neat dynamic. Where I tend to always think of Kate in a very hard and tough light, he always tends to think of Kate in a very vulnerable, feminine light. Together we've come to a place where we are mutually creating this character."

" *I think one of the reasons why Matthew and I have such natural chemistry onscreen, is that I am genuinely very taken by him when he is acting. He is a very captivating actor and I think Kate is supposed to be captivated by Jack.* "
— Evangeline Lilly

SURPRISE ME

Favorite season one twists, according to MATTHEW FOX...

"There were a bunch of them. I think what makes Damon [Lindelof] J.J. [Abrams], Carlton [Cuse] and Bryan [Burk] so amazing, and what's making our show so amazing, are the surprises. Yet so many of those surprises seem to make perfect sense and that's what's great. Finding out Locke was in a wheelchair and experienced a miracle was an incredible twist and really cool. It told you so much about how this man must feel about the island and in a really swift and concise way, you have a very deep understanding about why he would be seduced by the island first."

With a core cast in the double digits, *Lost* also provides the actors the luxury of working with a diverse group of performers that help shape their performance styles. As a newcomer, Lilly is soaking up the exposure to many acting approaches and she admits to being a keen observer of them all. "It's been a deliberate effort on my part to allow them to all be my teachers. One of the people that pops into my head is Yunjin Kim [Sun]. I have just been in awe with how she is able to bring *so* much to the screen doing so little. She's taught me what it means to be still as an actress and still portray a plethora of emotions and messages. Matthew [Fox] has taught me so much about being absolutely laid bare in front of the camera. I've learned a lot about what it means to be completely at ease and completely natural in front of the camera from Harold Perrineau [Michael]. I can go through and list every single actor and say the things that I've drawn from their performances and have tried to make my own."

LET IT BE WRITTEN

MATTHEW FOX **explains his script excitement…**

"I can't wait to read each script! I'm probably as excited or more excited to see each script than the audience is to see the next episode. I am an audience member on the script level, and I wait anxiously and with great excitement to see what is going to happen to all these people, and especially Jack."

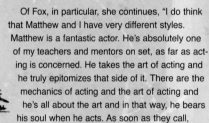

Of Fox, in particular, she continues, "I do think that Matthew and I have very different styles. Matthew is a fantastic actor. He's absolutely one of my teachers and mentors on set, as far as acting is concerned. He takes the art of acting and he truly epitomizes that side of it. There are the mechanics of acting and the art of acting and he's all about the art and in that way, he bears his soul when he acts. As soon as they call, 'Action!' the guy opens up like a cocoon and you see what's inside of him. When I was in that sew-up scene, I was so taken aback by him and this raw vulnerability that he showed, and what he was doing in the performance that he was giving, that it hindered me. I felt totally unable to meet him at that level! I did probably 50 takes of my coverage in that scene and couldn't nail it! I just couldn't get it. We had to come back a few weeks later and re-shoot the scene after I had acted with Matthew a little longer and had a rapport with him, and found a groove with him, and then I was able to do the scene.

"One of the things I've noticed working with all these actors, is that not only do they have different acting styles, but how drastically those acting styles rub off on you as an actor and how they affect your performance," Lilly continues enthusiastically.

"I think that's one of the reasons why Matthew and I have such natural chemistry onscreen, is that I am genuinely very taken by him when he is acting. He is a very captivating actor and I think Kate is supposed to be captivated by Jack."

Connecting with the rest of the *Lost* cast has been a huge plus for Fox too. "I really enjoy working with many different people on the show because you are defining these relationships between characters. Some of those relationships are a little bit more fun to play than others. I love the dynamic between Jack and Hurley [Jorge Garcia]. Hurley is sort of Jack's right hand man and is someone that will lighten Jack's emotional load because of his humor and how relaxed Hurley is. Towards the end of the first year, the dynamic between Jack and Locke, what Terry [O'Quinn] brings as an actor and the way we work with each other has been incredibly rewarding and challenging for me. My relationships with the actors on the show are defined by the dynamics of the characters. They are all very different, but I enjoy them all very much. There are a lot of different backgrounds and I've always loved how diverse and international the cast is. It's really exciting. Honestly, before I was on *Lost*, I was a huge fan of some of them, like Harold Perrineau. I remember doing my first scene with Harold, I was *so* excited – I'm a big fan of his. Those aspects of the show are really exciting; to come in and work with these people I had been a fan of for a while."

With 24 episodes of *Lost*'s first season to reflect back on, Fox and Lilly both easily identify moments they personally were most proud of. Fox offers, "The sequence where Jack revives Charlie [Dominic Monaghan] was really, really intense and the episode where Boone dies [*Do No Harm*] was something I'm incredibly proud of. I'm very, very proud of Ian Somerhalder and how he handled that whole situation, which isn't easy for an actor. Stephen Williams, who directed the episode was stellar and helped me go through something that was really difficult. I am really proud of the episode."

Speaking about Lilly, Fox is humble about his support of his leading lady. "If you are in the position that I am in on the show, and your female co-star has never really done much, you are going to definitely want to make her feel comfortable and relaxed. You do everything you can to make it fun and take a lot of the pressure off. One of the things Evangeline has handled so amazingly is the pressure of the whole thing. To be in that position without ever having experienced it on this scale takes a lot of courage and a lot of poise. She's always handled it quite well, and I just want to help her in any way I can and make sure nobody is getting in the way of it. Acting is ultimately like a dance and takes two people. One of the things that everybody on *Lost* understands about this process is that it takes a great amount of trust. When it works well, it requires both people to be participating – sort of 'feeling the other person out' through the process. It's something you need to be conscious of – that you have to be connected."

There are some big philosophical questions that Jack will have to come up against this year. The season premiere was a Jack episode and we got right into extending the philosophical divide between Jack and Locke."

— Matthew Fox

LOST

Lilly continues, "I think one of the Kate moments that stands out for me is near the end of the season when she gets into that rivalry with Sawyer [Josh Holloway]. They are at odds about who is going to be on the raft. There are two moments actually and they are in the same vein. One of them is when she turns on him suddenly and says, 'If I want your spot on the raft… I'll get your spot on the raft!' Basically in parenthesis, it could be 'I'll get your 'bleeping' spot!' she laughs. "Then at the end of the episode, when he comes to her by the fire to reconcile the situation, she basically shuts him down and says, 'You hurt me. You're out – period.' I think those moments were really significant because Kate started out as an impenetrable shell. She became something that was a little bit more approachable and more feminine, and I really felt she needed to end the season on a more rugged note, or re-run the risk that her character arc will be too fast. We've only been on the island for approximately 40 days. They say human beings need the minimum of 40 days to start or break a habit. Hers isn't just a habit, it's a way of living – being, thinking and feeling the way she does – and that's going to take a lot longer than 40 days to change."

SPIRITUAL PATH

EVANGELINE LILLY on her personal philanthropy…

"For me, that's something that has always been really personal and private. I'll be the first person to voice that everyone needs to get onboard and be helping where there is need, but I also like to keep the details closer to home, rather than putting it out in the press. I just like to hold them dear to my heart and allow them to be something I do on my own. I tend to keep the details private, but I absolutely believe that we all have a responsibility to those who have less than us. We all know that if we all just dropped our standard of living even by a degree, if every single one of us would do that, the world would be a very different place to live in."

Asked what she thought was Matthew Fox's best moment, Lilly smiles and says, "I think that Matthew's had some pretty spectacular moments to choose from. Probably the place where I saw some of his most incredible work was the entire amputation sequence of Boone's dying moments. He was just so desperate to save his life, and that entire event took place at the exact moment that Kate was forced to deliver Claire's baby in the jungle. That type of simultaneous action is one of my favorite things about *Lost*. That episode was quite spectacular and so momentous for the show, having the death, the birth and the crisis. I thought Matthew shone so brightly in that episode and showed so much darkness and depth. For me, it was so much fun to have Kate do something on her own. I loved playing that moment where I sit down and Jack looks so disturbed, and Kate comes out and looks so redeemed. She just glows when she sits down and says, 'How was your night? Are you ok?' It's always the other way around, with her in this dark place, so I really enjoyed that role reversal." In accord, Fox agrees that was his favorite Evangeline moment. "She handled the birthing of the baby really well and was really committed to that. You felt her reticence to get attached and involved on that kind of intimate level with somebody, and yet when she went there, she was really there. It was very strong work."

Now back to work on the second season of the series, both actors are very aware that this year audience members are hoping to see what will happen with the simmering romantic vibes going on between Kate and Jack, and Kate and Sawyer. Lilly has no clue where it's going herself, but she offers, "I try to analyze the situation as realistically as possible and I can only see Kate and Sawyer growing closer from what's happened. If Sawyer gets back to the island, they should have a new sense of value in each other. They say if you love something, let it go, and then see what happens from there. Not only did they break physically, but they really broke ties emotionally before they left. You see them both gazing out across the beach before they left, looking for each other, so they clearly still play a significant part in each other's lives. I also think that what Sawyer gives to Kate is a sense of normalcy and mutuality. When she is around Sawyer, suddenly who she is doesn't have to be hidden and I think she's less ashamed of it. I think she is more able to say, 'This is who I am. Take it or leave it, buddy!' That's a real gift. In real life, usually the people we feel the most in love with and attracted to are the people that allow us to be ourselves – faults and all. I think that for Jack, there is a certain amount of freedom and redemption he brings. He brings forgiveness, rather than acceptance. He keeps saying, 'I don't accept who you were, but I release you from it and

I accept who I believe you can be now, and that's a good person.' Those two gifts are equally as good, but they are just different."

Fox concurs and continues, "I think there is a huge, unknowable draw for Jack to Kate, but at the same time he needs her to grow up and become a more open, present and solid individual. She needs to stand for something a little bit more than she has so far. He feels she's manipulated and lied her way through a lot of the stuff she's tried to accomplish on the island. What he does know about her past – which is limited – completely fills out that picture, I just don't think that he trusts it. At the same time, it's there and so there's a real internal

> "I can go through and list every single actor and say the things that I've drawn from their performances and have tried to make my own."
> — Evangeline Lilly

Director of Photography Larry Fong with Evangeline Lilly

struggle within him and between the two of them. It's really interesting and the only way they will meet on a meaningful level is if there is some growth."

Aside from the triangle, Lilly and Fox also have other goals for their characters they hope they get to explore. Lilly says, "What I'm excited to see, as I think it will be a symbol both of healing and lack of healing, is for Kate to stand on her own two feet a little bit more. The first season, she spent a lot of time trotting behind Jack, following him like a loyal puppy dog – going where he went and helping in his endeavors, even if she didn't agree with him. For example, when he was trying to get people to go to the caves, she did not agree. Yet when he sits down and has a conversation with Sayid, and Sayid turns to Kate for her thoughts, she bows out and backs Jack up anway. So, I would really love to see her take on some of her own storylines and endeavors and set out her own goals. I think it's been right that she hasn't done that yet, because at this point, she is still focused on the horizon. She is still looking for rescue and a way out and she's not settled. I don't think that a person whose mind is elsewhere would be taking initiative on their own on the island, but I want to see her do that this season."

Fox has a shorter wish list, but he shares, "There are some big philosophical questions that Jack will have to come up against this year. The season premiere was a Jack episode and we got right into extending the philosophical divide between Jack and Locke. The title is *Man of Science, Man of Faith*. It's where we start the season and will be something that we continue this year.

"I know, at some point, Jack's really strict interpretation of the world based on science is going [to alter]. Given some of the things he's already experienced and witnessed with his own eyes, and more will be coming – Jack is going to have to be more open to the more magical elements.

"Philosophically, that's an amazing thing and in the dynamic between him and Locke, it's a really important issue. Otherwise, I just want to continue telling great stories. I think we had a great year last year. I think the writers learned a lot about what works and what doesn't. We learned a hell of a lot about that on a production level, so I think it was a real learning year for us. I just hope we continue to grow and raise the bar on ourselves, which is how I approach it.

"I know the writers are so excited about what they have in mind for this year. I'm just going to remain an audience member and find those things out script by script. I'll be loving that all the way along!"

BLOOPER ISLAND

EVANGELINE LILLY on *Lost*'s embarrassing moments...

"Oh, they happen all day! My feet are just getting wet, so I watch myself perform because I want to learn, but it's grueling! I watch and I get so embarrassed because I am constantly finding out that something just doesn't work, even something as simple as where I put my hands on my hips. Other times, the more devastating times are watching something and thinking I dropped the ball on the performance. This is the feeling I relate it to... when you are on your third date with a guy that you really like. You're really, really interested and all of a sudden you say something and you just think, 'I am a total moron! I can't believe I just said that! I am so bloody humiliated and embarrassed!' Then you go home and replay the night in your mind and you actually physically wince and let out little moans of embarrassment as you think about the things you did wrong. Well, that's exactly what it's like to replay scenes in my mind! It's just so hard to let go of those moments [laughs]!"

Dear Diary

" *Rain, magnificent sunsets, lightning storms — the list goes on and on...* "

"It's beautiful here. I've always loved Hawaii and I've been traveling here for a lot of years on vacation. My wife and I have always sort of joked about me getting a gig that would bring us here for an extended period of time — and here we are! The kids are incredibly happy and we are all very excited to be here.

I'm surfing a little bit again. I surfed in Southern California for a few years, but I gave it up because the water is so cold! Obviously, it's reinvigorated my desire to get back into surfing here. I brought my boards over and I try to get my kids involved.

As for shooting the show, every day is a new challenge. You've got rain, magnificent sunsets, lightning storms — the list just goes on and on. Working in a really natural environment as beautiful and majestic as Hawaii is amazing."

CREATURE FEATURES

Executive Producer BRYAN BURK, **Supervising Sound Editor** TOM DE GORTER, **Sound Designer** JACK GRILLO **and Visual Effects Supervisor** KEVIN BLANK **step out of the shadows and let us in on some secrets about the island's mysterious Monster…**

Steve LaPorte (Head of Make-up Department) adds some final touches to 'damaged Shannon' (Maggie Grace)

Of the laundry list of mysteries surrounding the survivors of *Lost* and that island they crashed on, there's really just one question that everyone is always asking, "What the heck is that 'Monster'?" Tromping around the island with a nasty disposition and one hell of a loud roar, the unseen 'Monster' is the terrifying unknown the audience is desperate to finally know. Is it a giant Kong-like gorilla? A cybernetic killing machine? Or maybe, co-star Dominic Monaghan got it right when he guessed, "An elephant with 17 cats sellotaped to it."

Have patience everyone, the truth will be revealed; Executive Producers J.J. Abrams, Damon Lindelof and Bryan Burk know exactly what that thing really is. Actually, there's an absolute method to their maddening plan of introducing the terrifying island entity one tiny clue at a time, some of which we can finally reveal for the first time…

First off, Executive Producer Bryan Burk explains the term 'Monster' is actually quite problematic. "We only refer to it as 'The Monster' in the office because it's a simple word. Publicly we never refer to it that way – whoever said it was a monster?" he smiles. "Cross out that T-Rex guess too," he says. "We knew from the beginning that it wasn't a dinosaur, so immediately we had to make sure anyone watching knew it wasn't a dinosaur. Knowing what 'IT' really was, we started working backwards to figure out how much to reveal, so that it wasn't too telling. We knew we were doing a series, so we didn't have to reveal everything in the first episode, but simultaneously we wanted the audience to have the tools to eventually figure out what it was. In this case, the tools were the sounds. All they had to do was listen.

"Some of our favorite films have *incredible* sound design and designers. Walter Murch [*Apocalypse Now*], Ben Burtt [*Star Wars* films], Gary Rydstrom [*Jurassic Park*] – these were guys whose contribution to their films undeniably made them riveting. Watch *Star Wars* with your eyes closed, and you'll really appreciate all the work [composer] John Williams and the sound designers put

into those films. Great sound design inspires us as much as any other art.

"Unfortunately, television has such a fast turnaround in Post-Production, there is rarely enough time to do proper sound design. In addition, we had a different challenge on *Lost*. How to create sounds for a 'Thing' that the audience wasn't going to see (at least in the short term). It had to be threatening – yet mysterious – and if done properly, would leave half the audience thinking it was organic – and the other half, man-made. I love nothing more in storytelling than ambiguity."

In the 24 episodes of *Lost's* first season, 'The Monster' (as we'll call it for the sake of this article) was never seen once. From its first introduction smashing through jungle palm trees in the pilot, to it attacking Jack and Locke with some telltale black smoke during the finale, 'The Creature' has been more 'sound' than substance. Tom de Gorter, Supervising Sound Editor on *Lost* and *Alias*, explains how the sound design initially started. "I met with J.J. and Bryan early on, even before they started shooting the pilot. One of the things they specified was that we weren't going to see this 'Creature'. It all had to be created through sound. You had to get the feeling of what it was doing even though you didn't see it and that is *the* most difficult part of dealing with sound effects. If you see something moving then that's easy. You know how big it is and what it sounds like, but we had none of that here. We were basically coming up with different sounds and seeing if they were appealing to Bryan and J.J. They specified that they wanted people to argue over the water cooler the next morning about whether it was actually mechanical or organic. We had to come up with effects that were neither or both. 'The Creature' is this ongoing evolution of sound, because it is constantly changing. Even in the original script, it said, 'It's a sound you've never heard before.'

"Originally, Paul Menichini was the Sound Designer on the pilot, of which there were two different versions – the pre-sell pilot and the one that went on the air," de Gorter continues. "Paul and I would talk and conceptualize and he would be sending sounds to Bryan and J.J. in Hawaii while they were shooting the pilot. They would listen to it on their computer and go, 'This is a cool sound' or 'I don't like this.' Bryan was very instrumental in the sound of 'The Creature', as much as any other Sound Designer on the show. So the original pilot timeframe was so tight – we were doing 36-hour shifts and going crazy at the time. We got through the original pilot and realized that there were certain things we wanted to change. During the summer, Bryan enlisted [Video Game Sound Designer] Jack Grillo [*Medal of Honor: Allied Assault*] to help out and add his take on the various sound

effects. Jack didn't cut anything for the show, but he was more the person that came up with concepts of sound – particularly for 'The Creature'. We integrated those into the actual show, by adding things here and there and mixing and matching Jack's raw sound effects." Burk continues, "At heart, we're all gamers over here. While film and television gets all the glory – some of the most brilliant, creative people are currently working in the gaming industry. The chance to work with Jack Grillo was an honor. His original and out-of-the-box approach to creating a world through sounds proved invaluable."

As the Additional Sound Designer for the *Lost* pilot, Jack Grillo was really charged with making the sound of 'The Monster' completely unique. "Bryan told me they had been living with this 'Monster' for such a long time, but they needed a fresh perspective," Grillo explains. "The idea was for me to come in for a month and shape the sound for this one element of the show. We talked through all the ideas they were looking for and I remember the strongest direction was not what it *was*, but what it *wasn't*. What that came to mean was that it couldn't sound 100% organic. There are plenty of things that make loud horrific sounds that aren't organic, so I was going for all kinds of metal creaking and latches and winches and dry ice squealing sounds. I experimented with a whole lot of different things." Burk adds, "What we are most excited about is the idea of people walking down the street and they hear a sound and possibly do a double-take because they heard something that will remind them of our show. That's not by accident."

De Gorter adds, "In the pilot, the character of Rose says [upon hearing 'The Creature']: "It sounds familiar. Someone asks, "Where are you from?" and she responds, "The Bronx." So Bryan Burk scoured New York City, looking for the perfect sound that we could incorporate into 'The Creature's' sound. It's there. Listen for it."

Grillo continues, "I went back and forth with Bryan a lot and because there wasn't a visual reference, it really became one of those things that eventually felt right. It was more about, "What combinations of sounds do what we want?" In the end, the sound of 'The Creature' to me doesn't sound like one thing."

With the pilot establishing the initial sound of the creature, the sound team used that to build upon as the season progressed. Tom de Gorter details the evolution saying, "Throughout the season, Mark Glassman was our Sound Effects Designer/Sound Editor. He cut all the sound effects in the show, including any additional 'Creature' design. 'The Creature' would change, again, as the action changed. If 'The Creature' was reaching down and grabbing someone, we had to come up with something different. It's an ongoing process."

BLACK ROCK MESSAGE

Supervising Sound Editor TOM DE GORTER on hiding clues within the sound design…

"It's always beneficial to know where [the story is] going because we can leave little clues and breadcrumbs so that people can follow along or look back and say, 'Oh yeah! We've heard that before.' We may not show our hand, but we like to leave a little bit. For example in the pilot [Part II], when the characters are listening to the French radio transmission, astute listeners would have heard 'I'm going to try and make it to the Black Rock.' Not only did Shannon *not* translate this, but we didn't even introduce the concept of the Black Rock for another six or seven episodes. I credit this foreshadowing and smart sound design to J.J. and Bryan."

"In the Season One finale, we showed a glimpse of the mysterious 'Thing' for the first time — a small wisp of black smoke trailing off into the jungle. As we reveal more of 'IT' in coming episodes, all of its bizarre sounds will begin to make sense." — Bryan Burk (Executive Producer)

L to R: Steve LaPorte
(Head of Make-up Department), Christine Lillo
(Additional Make-Up Artist), Maggie Grace (Shannon)

"At this point, I have been given a formal explanation [as to what the 'Thing' is], and there are elements that are so cool!"
— Kevin Blank
(Visual Effects Supervisor)

"Sound-wise, 'The Creature' is the hardest part of the show – and the show is no easy thing by any stretch of the imagination," de Gorter continues. "I'm very excited every time 'The Creature' comes out, because certain elements are always new and fresh and certain parts are constantly changing and that's the part I really love about it. 'The Creature' has really been a big part of the show, even in terms of our peers. We just won two Motion Picture Sound Editing Awards, which is equivalent to the SAG Awards or the DGA Awards. We won for best Sound Effects/Foley and ADR/Dialogue, which is very rare for one show to get both awards."

Of course, the sound design is great, but seeing is believing, too. The responsibility of bringing 'The Monster' to life, visually, falls to Kevin Blank, the Visual Effects Supervisor on *Lost.*. While audiences may be frustrated at their lack of knowledge about 'The Monster', imagine creating the visuals with no information. "In the very beginning, they were vague with me on what to do and I was sort of begging and pleading for more understanding. I felt I could offer more if I was in the loop. During the pilot I was given little tidbits, but yet, I still wouldn't say I was someone who had a clear picture of everything going on," he laughs. "The thing I wanted to know is, if I was King Kong, I would knock down trees one way and if I were a T-Rex, I would do it another way. If I was a big giant machine, I would do it another way, and that was never made clear. The next thing was, do we want to make trees that are so dense you can't see

anything or can you not see "IT" because there is a cloaking device or powers of invisibility? Again, these were things that weren't really given, initially. I found myself wishing there was a little bit of something on 'The Creature' that I could show, but J.J. *really* didn't want to do that. So at some point, we offered up some artwork that wasn't based on anything, other than 'let's be fans of the show and throw darts'. [The producers] were pretty set in their explanation, but we threw out a few things that were actually incorporated, like the smoky tendril in the finale."

Blank says the pilot was a magical experience due to the large budget and ample resources, but since *Lost* went to series, the team has had to get more creative with less. "There have been many, *many* 'Creature' things that have been scripted that were larger in scale and that had to be scaled back due to budget or resources. In *Walkabout*, we had a little bit of an extension of what we did in the pilot. In *Hearts and Minds*, Boone has a vision of 'The Monster' killing Shannon. At the last minute, they actually said they wanted to show 'The Monster' and we did a couple of things, but later it was yanked.

The thought was that we can show some of 'The Creature' – but since the episode was a visionquest, we could dismiss what we'd show as a dream. Ultimately, the decision was made that that was unfair to the audience and I was in agreement with that, so the only thing shown was oddly shaped shadows." In the meantime, Blank reveals he has since been included in the inner circle of those that know the truth behind 'The Monster'. "At this point, I have been given a formal explanation, and there are elements that are so cool!" he hints. Burk says audiences should expect "more reveals about 'The Monster' throughout season two." De Gorter adds, "It will definitely progress even further. I've hired a fourth Sound Designer, Mike Janescu, for season two, who has a lot of feature experience."

While 'The Creature' is a captivating character, Jack Grillo sums up the real success of this mysterious entity. "What surprised me was how little presence 'The Monster' had. I'm a fan of the show and I found myself not missing "IT". They did a nice job of not overdoing it and actually it's more impressive because of that. The show doesn't feel like it's all about 'The Monster', and that just makes the special effects the icing on the cake."

WINCHES & PULLEYS

Additional Sound Designer JACK GRILLO discusses his "monsters..."

"The crazy thing about putting it together was that I didn't know if it was one 'Monster' or several 'Monsters.' We really just played around. At one point, my wife was joking with me and said, 'Put in some roller coaster sounds.' Somehow it was in the back of my mind and I was collecting a bunch of winch and pulley sounds and put it together. About 10 minutes later, I realized, 'Hey, that sounds like a roller coaster!' Oddly enough, that was the stuff Bryan [Burk] really responded to."

BETWEEN A ROCKER AND A DARK PLACE...

Abduction. Addiction. Just two of the many trials that have tested Charlie and Claire's strength and sanity since they found themselves stranded on the island. Throughout their personal struggles, the two have remained close. **DOMINIC MONAGHAN** and **EMILIE DE RAVIN** talk about how they got *Lost*…

> "*I really liked the Charlie flashback in The Moth where he is on stage with his brother singing... We had a whole bunch of girls at the front of the stage, you're wearing tight jeans, doing your Spinal Tap moves — you can have fun with that [laughs].*"
>
> — Dominic Monaghan

How would you describe your flashback – the events that led you to *Lost*?

Dominic Monaghan: I'd been living in LA since 2001, hanging out, and getting an American manager, agent, and all that kind of stuff. We'd wrapped on *The Lord of The Rings* in 2003, and then I did a film in New York, and two films in England. One was called *Spivs* with Ken Stott, which was fun, and then I did this other thing called *The Purifiers*, a rough remake of *The Warriors*.

Emilie de Ravin: I've lived mainly here in LA for the last five years, but do go home [to Australia], periodically. I did a show for a couple of years when I first moved out here, and then was working on and off on a couple of shows and films. I wasn't really looking to do a pilot last year – there was nothing that interested me and I was very happy to be working up in Edmonton and avoiding pilot season during that time. And then I heard about *this*, which sounded very interesting…

DM: Coming up to pilot season, my agent called me and said, "Do you wanna do pilot season?" I didn't really know what that was, so he explained that it's essentially where they make first episodes of shows to see if they get picked up. I said, "Well… I'm not really that keen on getting back into television," because I'd done television in England, and I was a little disappointed and despondent with the industry. So he said, "Fine, OK – unless there's something really great coming up, then we'll not include you." I'd read a couple of scripts that were OK, nothing that fantastic, and then he sent me the first season of *Alias*. I watched it, called him up and said, "Thanks… what was that all about?" and he said, "Well, the creator of the show, J.J. Abrams, is creating this new show called *Lost*. As of yet, there's not a part in there for you, but they're not casting in the usual way."

EDR: There was no script, nothing really. [With me] I spoke to casting and spoke to J.J. [Abrams], sent a tape down and got cast off that! It was the quickest, strangest, easiest casting process I've ever been through [laughs]! I shouldn't say *easiest* though, as it was much *harder* in that respect – sending a tape off and just getting cast off that doesn't give you anything to work with. You don't know what they want – you don't know whether they're saying, "No, try it this way."

DM: I went and met J.J. Abrams, Damon Lindelof, Bryan Burk, and April Webster, who was casting it. At this point, Charlie was a 45 year-old English rocker, who'd been through the mill. My pitch was, "Wouldn't it be more interesting if this person was a young kid, who'd had the smallest amount of success and then the carpet had been ripped out from under him? He'd have all this frustration and ambition that had gone nowhere." Whereas, when you're 40, and you've got a bit of money and you think, "Oh well, I've done it – I've had my day." So I went away, called my agent and said, "Whatever we need to do to pursue this, we should, because it looks really good." When I came in again, Charlie was becoming more like the character that we had spoken about, and it was like a collaboration of ideas.

EDR: I had a lot of nerves – not having met any [of the team] prior to [this], and I'd never been to Hawaii, either. So, I flew to Hawaii, met everyone, and it turned out great! Everyone's really, *really* helpful and nice, and the cast got along pretty much instantly.

The premise of the show sounded very unlike television, which I guess is what really made me sit up and listen. I didn't have much interest doing television necessarily, but I've loved J.J.'s work in the past. There was an instant respect to make me go, "OK, this could be really cool." One of the things with TV is that you're limited in a way – being the same person every day. But when you've got a cast like this, there's so many different relationships to develop and people to work with – I think that's a huge plus.

ORIGINS OF A ROCK STAR

DOMINIC MONAGHAN on creating Charlie…

"I based his look and his attitude at the audition on a kind of Richard Ashcroft – the guy from The Verve – and a more diluted version of Liam Gallagher from Oasis… but Liam with a sense of comedy. I think Liam's very funny, but he doesn't know it. His whole attitude is hilarious.

"I think a lot of actors have aspirations to be singers or lead guitarists in bands. On stage is a powerful place to be. If you've done any theatre/stage work, you'll understand that power. I have mates who are in a band in Manchester. The band used to be called Lift,

but it's now called Magic Torch. I'd go to their sound-checks and practices and pick up a tambourine – I like that. I've sung Oasis tunes at parties and sung at wrap parties, too. I'm not under any illusions that I have a good enough voice to be a singer, but what I'm able to do – because of the experience I've had – is not be scared on stage in front of a large audience. It's fun.

"I really liked the Charlie flashback in *The Moth* where he's on stage with his brother singing, We had a whole bunch of girls at the front of the stage, you're wearing tight jeans, doing your Spinal Tap moves – you can have fun with that [laughs]."

Did any of your previous outdoors experiences help prepare you to work on this show?

DM: I think there's a genuine 'pacific island feel' to, certainly the South Island of New Zealand [where *Rings* was filmed], and Hawaii, Fiji – those kind of places. I understood some of the myths and legends and their respect for the land, ocean, sky, and the mountains.

EDR: I like camping and I love the outdoors so I had no problem with that. It's actually a breath of fresh air to be able to go to work somewhere so beautiful and fresh – not like working in Downtown LA where you're outside, but you may as well not be [laughs]!

DM: Working on a big ensemble cast [on *Rings*] was key, for me, and I think still is key. Ultimately, the thing that I brought to the table was I know what it means to be working in a large group of people, so I kept that in my mind.

EDR: Overall, being able to go to a gorgeous beach and work is one of the big pluses. It does get a little hot sometimes, and there are many bugs in the jungle, but it's all worth it. The bites are worth it [laughs]!

What aspects of *Lost* do you find the most intriguing?

EDR: I think Locke in general. I'm really, *really* interested to find out more, I always have been. I love his character, and I think that Terry plays him to a 'T'. Locke's the guy that you want to trust. He seems to know everything, he's this sweet nice guy who brings us all food and has so many talents, and is just a very intelligent person. But there's just something going on there. There's something *more* there, and I think that is one of the most intriguing things to me. What is his zeal?

DM: I like what Locke symbolizes – this kind of serene god-like character – someone who has the knowledge that we don't have yet.

I've really enjoyed Walt's story, too. Malcolm's a really great friend of mine. For a young actor to have performed like that with a bunch of people – some who have worked for 30 years in this industry – is amazing. To not only hold his own, but to put in one of the performances of the year, has been fantastic to watch. You look at a character like that, and you

"What I'm trying to play is a bad good guy. He's a good guy — but there's a badness to him. At some points he thinks, 'Have to be good! Have to be good!'"

– Dominic Monaghan

think, "He'll be the defenceless kid who everyone has to help out," but he may have this telepathic/ESP-type power that you can see at some points. I'm very intrigued by that.

Emilie – how challenging was it to act as a pregnant character?
EDR: You get used to it – I didn't have heavy clothing on over the top so it wasn't too bad. But it's definitely nicer not wearing that anymore [laughs]! I made my own notes as well. You need to be aware that she wouldn't sit certain ways – she wouldn't be able to sit up straight on the beach, because she's so extremely pregnant. There are things you have to think about like that to really make it believable. I've never been pregnant myself – so I did a lot of research, and talked to a lot of people.

How was the actual birth scene?
EDR: Even people who have had children themselves have said, "Your mind makes you forget it to certain extent – otherwise you'd probably never have anymore children [laughs]!" So everyone told me, "I don't know how I'd recreate that – even having had children myself!" It's also such a personal thing. Everyone is so different. For some people it's so easy, and depending on your body shape, the size of the baby, if you've had children before, and just you as a person – some people have the easiest births, and some people are in labor for days! It's just one of those things you have to just make choices with. We had an OBGYN [a nurse] on set to talk about it, too. We timed everything out and really just made it as gritty and as real as possible as opposed to one of these 'TV births' where they forget about the umbilical cord and it's all clean and cute and cuddly [laughs]!

One for the cast's Mancunian – do you help the creative team with the little British quirks and details?

DM: Yeah – there's a lot of "bloody", "sodding" and a lot of generic English stuff which a Mancunian wouldn't say. They tend to 'posh-out' their English people, assuming we're all, "Oh gosh… my goodness… flipping heck!" like Hugh Grant [laughs]. I'm like, "My mates wouldn't say that – *Mancunians* wouldn't say that." They would say, "Bloody hell" every so often, but they don't say it as much as they want Charlie to say it. So they have to be careful of that [laughs].

Some of the clothes are a little [off] – they've wanted to put me in cravats and ties every so often in my flashbacks. So yeah, I help 'em out with things like that.

We did a scene in a pub in a Charlie flashback, and they were giving people glasses of beer. I was like, "It's not glasses of beer… it's an English pub so it's got to be pints." You wouldn't have an English guy sit with his mate drinking half a pint of beer – and he certainly wouldn't be drinking half a pint of beer in a glass [laughs]! If anything, he'd say, "Can I have half a pint…in a pint glass [laughs]!" I've asked them to put jars of Marmite in cupboards when we've been in houses too, little English things like that. There was a scene where we had a cup of tea – I come in late at night with a girl, and the initial thing was we were gonna have a glass of wine. I said, "You might have a glass of wine, but chances are, he'd have a can of beer. If they didn't have beer, she'd give him a cup of tea." Englishy stuff like that.

"There was no script, nothing really… I spoke to casting and spoke to J.J. [Abrams] , sent a tape down and got cast off that! It was the quickest, strangest, casting process I've ever been through [laughs] !"

– Emilie de Ravin

BIRTH

EMILIE DE RAVIN on "just going for it"…

"You want to be in the moment for something like that. Giving birth is not a planned event, so I think it's better to be 'spur of the moment'. Doing that was a lot of fun and I enjoy being able to do something that's not easy, as opposed to just going to work and just being yourself, which some [acting] jobs require you to do. This was something that enabled me to do a lot of research."

What other aspects of this show have surprised you so far?

DM: I liked how they juxtaposed Charlie being an addict, and Charlie making a decision to stop being an addict just as this responsibility of Claire and the baby came along. Claire symbolizes a place that he wants to be in his life. Maybe protecting a young girl and taking care of her baby will actually bring him out of himself – the addict will kind of disappear a little bit. I thought that was a nice journey to go on.

EDR: One of my original quandaries was, "This could end up being really boring – we're on an island!" [laughs] But I found out – before we even started – that this island is not a normal island, which pretty much gives [the writers] complete artistic freedom to do whatever they want to do, which is great! With this show, you seriously never know. There hasn't been one boring moment on the show yet [laughs]!

FORMING FRIENDSHIPS

Claire and Charlie obviously have a connection. **DOMINIC MONAGHAN** and **EMILIE DE RAVIN** discuss their *other* close allies…

DM: In the early days Charlie had some connection with Jack and Kate, because they make that decision not to tell anyone what happened to the co-pilot.

EDR: Claire doesn't really trust anyone completely. But I think that [she trusts] Kate, from having the birthing experience with her. And I think she – not *automatically* trusts – but does trust Jack, as he has had high involvement with her pregnancy, too.

DM: I think Charlie sees something similar in Hurley, too – someone who's at a weird transition in their life. He isn't afraid to say that he's scared, or unsure. He isn't trying to be the big hero.

> " I get the impression that coming into season two, there'll be a palpable split in the group, with characters fighting for space, territory, water and food. "
>
> – Dominic Monaghan

What would you like season two to bring for your characters?

EDR: I think season two will be interesting for her. Being pregnant, and not being able to do as many things when your pregnant [beforehand] – it's a little bit different now she's actually had the child. In the show's time, she's only just had the child, less than a week ago. How is she gonna deal with that? Her development as a mother, as a person and how that changes your life completely will be interesting – especially as she wasn't actually planning on being a mother.

DM: There's a nice human edge to Charlie. I like how the writers have quite bravely said, "One of our main characters is screwed up and is able to show it." Clearly all the characters are screwed up, but Charlie holds his hand up and says, "I'm in a mess," and I like that. But I'd like to see Charlie grow a little bit in terms of taking some responsibility. He's been helping people out quite a lot this season, but he's not actually seen a problem and faced it on his own. He'll be forced to readdress his addictions – these ugly ghosts that seem to follow Charlie around. I'd like him to find himself in a situation where he's having to think about his issues with faith and trust, too.

EDR: Claire can mingle with people and be more a part of the group now. I think she's really going to break out of her little shell, form new relationships with people, enemies, friendships, whatever that may be – it's definitely going to be exciting! Somebody may be able to help with that, and then she can go off and be her own body and her own self. "Season two – Claire's adventures in the wild [laughs]!"

DM: I get the impression that coming into season two, there'll be a palpable split in the group, with characters fighting for space, territory, water and food. I've been talking to the writers since day one, and I'd like for Charlie to remain neutral. When I went in for my second audition, I started talking about Iago – the character from *Othello*. He's like Wormtongue in *Rings* – he's supposed to be Othello's confidente, but what he's doing is winding up Othello to act out things he wants to happen. I would like to be in that position... and then get discovered – for both of those groups to go, "You know what – screw you man."

> *"Being able to go to a gorgeous beach and work is one of the big pluses. It does get a little hot sometimes, and there are many bugs in the jungle, but it's all worth it. The bites are worth it [laughs]!"*
>
> — Emilie de Ravin

Charlie (Dominic Monaghan) with rocker brother Liam (Neil Hopkins)

RETROSPECTIVE

DOMINIC MONAGHAN on the power of the flashbacks…

"My favorite Charlie bits are where he goes into himself. There's a scene in the pilot where Kate says to him, 'You're a nice guy.' She walks off, and Charlie just stops and goes into this place where he remembers taking heroin on the plane and obviously what Kate said resonates with him – he's thinking, 'No I'm not.' He wants to be a nice guy. What I'm trying to play is a bad good guy. He's a good guy – but there's a badness to him. Maybe that twists at some points, that the bad guy leads him and he thinks 'Have to be good! Have to be good!'"

Left: To the right of Emilie de Ravin – Nick Jameson (the psychic Richard Malkin), and crew members Dan Lipe (red shirt), John Mumper (grey shirt) and Rick Tiedemann (behind the camera)
Above: Claire's reading from the psychic Richard
Right: Claire's former boyfriend Thomas (played by Keir O' Donnell)

THE OTHERS

Can you talk us through exactly how yourself and J.J. came up with *Lost*?

Damon Lindelof: ABC basically wanted to do the 'Survivors' of drama – 'a plane crashes on an island in the south pacific and the show is about what happens next.' I think both J.J. and I had the concern that that wasn't really a TV show. It was a good idea for a movie, maybe a mini-series, but it didn't feel like that premise could sustain multiple episodes. We didn't know where the stories would be coming from – once they got their food and water, and after the basic survival, there wouldn't be much left. We both came to the conclusion fairly early on – at first, independently of each other, and then when we first met – that if the island they crashed on was this strange and mysterious place, and if the people who were on the plane were even *more* strange and mysterious than the island, then you would actually have a lot of story material. That was the principal jumping-off point.

J.J. is a great lover of *The Twilight Zone*, that's the show that he's obsessed with and I've seen them all as well. I love science fiction, I grew up on it, so both of us definitely had that sensibility. It was the first thing we started talking about. We said, "That's the show we want to do – focus on 'character'." Why they are here, what they are going to be doing, these are the questions that led to the construction of a very large ensemble cast.

There were actors who we really liked but who weren't right for the part they were reading for and we said, "Let's just write a character for them!" like Yunjin Kim who [originally] went for Kate. We loved her so much that an idea occurred to us – Yunjin speaks fluent Korean, and we thought what we could change the idea we had of an elderly Japanese couple who didn't speak English to a young Korean couple, and so we cast her. We saw Jorge Garcia in an episode of *Curb Your Enthusiasm*, and just said, "We love that guy. He has to be on our show."

Genesis

Co-Creator/Executive Producer DAMON LINDELOF looks back to the origins of the island and discusses how the show came to be…

We were changing our minds all the way through the process. We were going to kill Jack initially. Stephen McPherson, who was running Touchstone then and and now runs ABC, told us that that would be a huge mistake. He said that the viewers of the show would feel very alienated by us killing a major character half-way through the pilot, and you know what? He was right. So we changed our minds…

A lot of the actors came in and read sides for other characters, because we didn't have sides for the character that they wanted to read for. Jorge came in and read Sawyer's sides. Matthew read for both Sawyer and Jack, and Yunjin, as I mentioned, read for Kate. Harold Perrineau was the only person who ever read for Michael, we just wanted him. What happened was, we would end up talking to the actors, for example, Harold, saying, "Tell us about yourself." He said things like, "I'm doing this play… I'm married…" So we heard him talk and were like, "Wow – let's write this kind of stuff for Michael!" We were taking stuff from their lives as people, and fusing the characters to them. It became very collaborative.

Charlie was written to be a has-been rock star who was in his mid-to-late 40s, who had this Spinal Tap-like career, but now it's over. Dominic came in, and it was like, "What if he's just a one-hit wonder and his career's over but he doesn't realize it yet?" A lot of Charlie's humor came from Dominic, and certainly his sense of personal style. Every actor that we met – because the script wasn't written yet – began to inspire character levels as we were casting them. We'd say, "Let's write to *that* person as opposed to writing it as we wanted to and having the actor force themselves into a role that might not make sense to them."

It all happened so fast from that first meeting that J.J. and I had with each other, which was just two days after ABC came in and said we want you to do this show. I think it was 11 weeks later we handed them the two-hour pilot, cut, mixed and everything. In that time we cast it, wrote it, shot it, cut it…

As the Island is a really important character, how hard was it to find the right island?
Really early on, the only places that were in play for viably shooting a television show were New Zealand and Hawaii. We needed to go some place that had an infrastructure – equipment and a local crew who knew what they were doing. New Zealand, obviously because of Peter Jackson and what had started with the *Hercules* and *Xena* shows, they'd trained an indigenous crew how to do the shows. But with New Zealand, the time issue was a big deal. How long it took to get there, sending film back, the time difference, and also, more importantly, New Zealand was much more foresty. We were looking for something more jungley, because the island was supposed to be an island in the south pacific. So, if you're going to shoot an island in the south pacific… go to an island in the south pacific, so that's Hawaii [laughs]! The rub there was that there were three other shows at the time that were already shooting on the island. We were last in, and got sort of what was left behind, the remnants of what the other shows weren't using. I think that ended up making the show… we had to work that much harder and it was that much sparser. J.J. really just directed the hell out of it.

What do you recall about shooting the pilot episode?
The first thing is that the guys in Hawaii, the crew that we have, were very savvy about shooting in Hawaii, and were very in tune with the rapid weather changes. It would rain, but it would only rain for 20 minutes. So you would just figure out where to go or what to shoot while it was raining. The big sort of 'set' in the pilot was the beach, and we were just blessed with enormously great weather for the majority of time we were there. Our *studio* had the natural light. The most tricky part was sound – we were by the ocean, but we had an awesome sound guy.

The good news was that we had about five weeks in Hawaii to shoot the two-hour pilot, so there was some breathing space to do things the right way. We would set up the cockpit in the jungle, go and shoot at that location, and what you didn't get in one day you came back and got the next day. Sarah Caplan, who produced it, I give her all the credit of figuring out how to shoot a show, a pilot, with no sets.

There is that memorable cloud burst in the pilot…
A lot of that stuff we did shoot the first day. There were sporadic thunderstorms, but you have to match the intensity of the rain in every shot. For at least two days we were shooting that run through the jungle with the monster chasing them and the majority of that rainstorm was manufactured by the special effects crew, and I mean a couple of guys were standing in some rain towers. They knew just what they were doing.

And from the first ever episode to season one's epic effectively three-hour finale…
Initially, the plan was we were just going to do a two-part season finale, so that it would be a total of two hours and would run over concurrent weeks. Then ABC asked us to do a 90-minute episode for the second part of it and we overwrote it, so we just ended up with three hours. We felt that that was the amount of screen time that this story needed. At first it was very overwhelming, but then we realized that this was a really great opportunity to really do all the things that we wanted to do. There are 14 major characters, and we wanted to give them all compelling stories to explore. Every single character on the show was going to get a flashback – everything just went so fast, we were all exhausted.

"J.J. really just directed the hell out of it."

I didn't really go to Hawaii as much as I would have liked to. Very quickly, I realized that I needed to be in LA more than there. Over the course of the first season, I think I only went to Hawaii four or five times. Jack Bender, our producing director, runs our show in Hawaii so Carlton spends a lot of time with him. But it's such a well-oiled machine, it doesn't require my physical presence.

"Shooting outside, we are slaves to the weather."

Your role on the show must involve a huge amount of multi-tasking on a day-to-day basis…
It's different every day. It starts with a meeting in the Writers' Room where we basically talk about the concept of a given episode. We usually say, "Who's episode is it going to be? What's the flashback story that we want to tell, etc?" We have fairly detailed ideas of who these characters were in their past lives. So, we'll say [for example] "It's time to tell the story of how Locke got in his wheelchair." Then we'll say, "OK, what's happening on the island that will emotionally illustrate that story?" Then we literally begin to build the story. Once it's all up on the board, which is a process that usually takes about three or four days per episode, sometimes five, the writer of that episode will then go off and do a fairly detailed outline scene by scene. Carlton [Cuse] and I read the outline and make notes, and then the writer goes off and does another pass (obviously if the writer and I are writing the episode, we write our own outlines and notes for each other). The writer then goes off and actually writes the script for that

episode, and by the time that's happening, the room starts again on the *next* episode, so the overlap begins. So, at any given time, once we're up and running, there is: a script being written, at the same time that another episode is being broken, another outline is being written and another episode is being cut [laughs]! So *all* those things are going on. Carlton and I get in every morning, sit down on the couch, eat our breakfast and say, "Right, here's the game plan today: you go in a room and start working on an episode, you can go into the editing room and fix this thing, then we'll reconvene before lunch." But it's different every time. My focus is that I spend a lot of my time in the Writers' Room.

Outside of filming *Lost*, living on the island must bring lots of opportunities for the cast and crew to experience unique and relaxing Hawaiian things…
I hope that the cast has had that opportunity now that they've been there for a season. It really is hard work though, and on days that they're not shooting, they're also doing a lot of press. The good news is that when they go to bed at night and wake up in the morning they're in Hawaii! A lot of them live right by the water, and it's just a beautiful place. But when we were shooting the pilot we were shooting six day weeks. We would wrap eight o'clock on a Saturday night, everyone would stagger back to their hotel rooms and sleep for 14 hours. On Sunday we'd all go and see a movie together, and then on Monday we were back shooting again. Because there aren't any sets, and we're shooting outside almost exclusively, we are slaves to the weather.

Have any story threads been changed/dictated because of how the weather has been?
The beach that we had the wreckage on, when winter came, the waves on the North Shore get really big. Our set was going to get washed away, so we wrote it in to the show. They've settled on another beach – and that's because we had to do that. We would love to have had them hanging around the wreckage a little longer than they actually did. But it was good because it signified a step forward in their evolution on the show – moving beyond the crash, and moving the show into another mode of storytelling.

LOCKE DOWN

Of all the characters, John Locke was the only one planned from the get-go, explains DAMON LINDELOF...

"Locke was in there. Nobody came in and read for Locke. We said, 'There should be a guy on the island who is sort of mystical and quiet, and this is the best thing that ever happened to him.' Originally, we wanted to get Scott Glenn to play that part, even though we hadn't really written anything for him yet. He got offered this other pilot at CBS, so he went and did that. Then, we were in Hawaii on a location scout, with Sarah Caplan, J.J. and myself. I can't remember who it was that said, 'Hey, what about Terry – Terry O'Quinn in *Alias*?' and J.J. literally picked up the phone and called Terry and said, 'Hey, I'm doing this pilot, this new show – do you want to be in it?' Terry said, 'Sure.' J.J. was like, 'Do you not even want to know what it is or who you're playing?' and Terry was like, 'No, I trust you.'"

Of all the mysterious forces that we've experienced in the first season, which do you find the most intriguing?

To be honest with you, I think 'The Monster' has always been less interesting to me than a lot of the other things. At the end of the day, whatever complicated explanation you come up with for what it is, it is this thing that is in the jungle that kills people. Eventually we'll show you something, you'll see it, and you'll say, "That's what it is!" and you'll be done, but things like the hatch represent such greater mysteries. Even if we were to go inside, see what there is and experience that, you still wouldn't necessarily know who put it there, who built it there, what its purpose was. Are there other hatches like it on the island? Are they all connected? It's the difference between movies and TV – TV goes on and on, and movies just end.

"OK, this isn't even science fiction," so you buy it.

I feel like that kind of thing on *Lost* is cool, because the audience that watches the show, the people who want it to be supernatural can say this is a very weird island, and the people who want it to be natural, can dismiss the supernatural phenomena. Like, "Jack's not *really* seeing his dead father – he just hasn't slept in three days. He's extremely stressed and he feels guilty, and no one else sees his dead father." But then I'd be like, "How do you explain that by following that 'ghost' he's actually located the coffin… and water – which is what everybody else is seeking?" There's this magic feel to *Lost* without ever actually showing the magic. That kind of stuff really appeals to me. I loved M. Night Shyamalan's *The Sixth Sense*, and *Unbreakable*, especially. I'm a huge comic book junkie. [In *Unbreakable*] that idea of seeing an origin story of a superhero has that sense of magic. That world [Shyamalan created] is so convincing to me, that way [Bruce Willis' character] has super strength and the way he experiences it and realizes it is so real.

Something that J.J. said to me very early on – and I'm sure he's said it before he'd even heard of *Lost* – is that he's attracted to 'B' concepts done 'A'. Like *Alien* or *Jaws*, those are 'B' movie ideas. The way that the writers, directors, actors and everybody involved with those movies approached the material was that it wasn't just about a shark, or it wasn't just about an alien. When we decided to do the show, we just said it's very important that we really take it seriously. All the characters on the show are reacting to things the way that you and I would react if we were in a scenario like this.

season two on *every* level is: Who are The Others? If you were one of these 'other' people, whoever they are, how would you view the survivors of the

KATE: THE ORIGINAL HEROINE

DAMON LINDELOF explains how, in the show's early stages, Evangeline Lilly's character was destined to be the central hero of *Lost*…

"She was not originally constructed to be a fugitive. Her story was that she had just gotten married, but she was really regretting it. She was with this guy that she probably shouldn't have married. They were flying back from Australia where they were honeymooning and he was going to the bathroom in the back of a plane when the crash occurred. Her series-long arc would've been trying to get reunited with her husband, and in the meantime, falling in love with either Sawyer or Jack, but that changed too."

SINS 8

THE FATHER

Both have had loved ones ripped away from them. Both have come close to death on the island. JOSH HOLLOWAY and HAROLD PERRINEAU, talk about the dynamics Sawyer and Michael bring to *Lost*…

> *"Michael and Walt, who have these titles of father and son, are the biggest strangers of all. They have no idea who the other person is even though they have these titles which suggest they know each other intimately."*
>
> — Harold Perrineau

Boarding

Oceanic Airlines flight 815, Michael Dawson could never have anticipated the plane would hit turbulence, plummet from the sky, and crash on a remote Pacific island. As one of the survivors, he has since struggled to protect his son Walt from the unknown and bizarre mysteries that surround them. Millions of viewers and six Emmy Awards later, actor Harold Perrineau, who plays the part of Michael, admits he never fathomed *Lost* would become such a phenomenon.

"I really didn't," says Perrineau, who graciously agreed to do this interview at 7:30am on his day off. "I thought it was a really good show and my wife was like 'I think this is going to be the biggest show ever.' And I kept going 'What does that mean?' And she's like 'the biggest show ever.' And I am like 'What does that mean? Ever... as in the history of TV?' She really believed it, so I was like, 'Right on!' I had no idea and I thought maybe I'd get a year or two out of it. I have a long history of doing shows that are critically acclaimed but not a lot of people are watching them. I thought it may be like that, but who knew?"

Perhaps the casting agents who amassed the large ensemble of talented actors... *Lost*'s popularity can at least be partially attributed to their amazing chemistry which naturally fell into place.

"The only way I can explain it is the parallels of what is going on in the show, and what is going on with the island, is true," offers Perrineau. "We are sort of secluded on the island together. We're all actors, all here doing the show, and all feeling a lot of the same pressures of doing publicity and getting our work done. In that sense, we all get each other because we are all in a similar boat. We all have to stick together and be there for each other in the exact same way they are forced to on *Lost*. If we were in Los Angeles, we could all go our separate ways."

Did the infamous midnight skinny dipping help them bond as well? "No comment," laughs Perrineau.

Unlike Perrineau, Michael can be a bit rough around the edges but who can blame him? A New York artist and construction worker, Michael has only a few days with Walt after picking him up in Australia, where he was being raised by his recently deceased mother. Although family, the two had not interacted in several years and it was that fractured relationship which immediately roped Perrineau in.

"I'm always curious about people – who they are supposed to be in the world vs. who they actually are," he explains. "These people are all on this island and they are all strangers. But Michael and Walt, who have these titles of father and son, are the biggest strangers of all. They have no idea who the other person is even though they have these titles which suggest they know each other intimately. The journey to either get rid of those titles or really fulfill them was interesting to me."

As he screams 'Walt!' amidst the chaos and plane wreckage in the pilot, it is evident he has an unconditional love for his son and is trying to live up to his parental duties. A tad overprotective, many of Michael's decisions seem based on Walt.

"They definitely do," agrees Perrineau. "Most of what Michael does is about his son and fulfilling this idea of a father. As we go along, we get to see how much he's always wanted to do that and what he gave up, and this chance to get it back. I'd say 90 per cent of what he does is about his son. Walt definitely defines who Michael is."

Not all the central figures are so selfless though. Enter James "Sawyer" Ford, a sexy, rugged con man none of his co-survivors trust and viewers love to hate. With a flare for pushing people's buttons, stashing items, shooting his mouth off, and getting into trouble, Sawyer's tough guy façade has made him one of the most compelling characters to watch. Did you know that co-stars Matthew Fox and Dominic Monaghan even originally auditioned for the savory role?

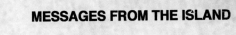

"What jumped out about Sawyer's character to me was his brutal honesty and that he wasn't a pleaser," offers Josh Holloway. "I was just ready to play that type of character."

Although Holloway appears to be an overnight success, the Georgia native began as a model before racking up credits on *Angel*, *CSI*, *The Lyon's Den* and the indie films *Cold Heart* and *Dr. Bunny*. Despite a down-to-earth and personable reputation, Holloway says delving into his bad boy side wasn't a stretch.

"It's quite easy," he grins. "About eight years of rejection has made Sawyer easy to find."

Being a dedicated father in real life has also given Perrineau a unique perspective on his character.

"As a parent, in the very beginning, it made it a little difficult to play him," he acknowledges. "I had to let go of all of my parental understanding because Michael didn't have that. Sometimes I felt it got in my way and other times my personal experience enabled me to get the depth of what he might be feeling. If my child was taken from me in the middle of the night by some guys who looked like they were from the movie *Deliverance*, I'd lose my mind."

That ability to draw on past experiences can be invaluable since out of the starting gate, it has all been a big guessing game. And we're not just speaking about the crazy French woman, Danielle, the 'monster,' cursed numbers, or the ominous, the Others. Creators J.J. Abrams and Damon Lindelof have kept the actors relatively bewildered about their characters' colorful, and often checkered, histories.

MORTALITY PLAY

JOSH HOLLOWAY and **HAROLD PERRINEAU** discuss how on *Lost*, things can become a matter of life or death out of the blue…

Death has come knocking a few times on *Lost*. Last season, Boone was killed and this year, his sibling Shannon raises the body count. The only person who has job security on this show is The Grim Reaper.

"Yes, at times it can be unsettling knowing your character could be killed," sighs Josh Holloway. "However, that's the nature of the business. Pilots don't get picked up. Shows get cancelled. Characters get killed/written off. As far as for the cast goes, it is hard to say goodbye to such amazing people but real friendships remain."

Harold Perrineau echoed similar sentiments when it was announced someone would bite the dust last season. "You worry for a little bit and then stop," he explains. "Not because I thought it won't be me but at some point, I didn't want to think about it anymore. I wanted to do my job and if it was me, that is fine because that is life as an actor. I think of *Lost* as part of a long, and hopefully, continuing career. But no matter who it was, it would have been shocking."

LOST

> " I really want
> to know the deal
> about the Others.
> I'm really confused
> about them. "
> — Harold Perrineau

"None of it was mapped out," explains Perrineau. "I really just knew the obvious about this father and son, but didn't know why Michael hadn't seen him. I started guessing and for a while explored that not only did he have no idea what to do with his son, but had no real inclination to do anything. We explored it in an episode when we're playing golf and Michael completely forgot about Walt. 'Oh right, I left you somewhere.' Not too much was laid out and I think there was a combination of what I was doing and what they were writing that defined who Michael is. When we first see him, he was dressed very corporate with khakis, buttoned down shirt, and a nice watch. There's a typical sort of African American corporate sound where the guy is extremely articulate and I didn't want to give him that. When I made that choice, they adopted 'he's not corporate but he's trying to be.'"

Michael's past unfolded in the episode *Special* which detailed his artistic aspirations, personal setbacks, breakup with his partner Susan, and being hospitalized after being hit by a car. This season in *Adrift*, Michael fought for custody of Walt before relinquishing him to his estranged wife, resulting in a tearful farewell. After all the wait, Perrineau was thrilled about his character's back-story. "It fulfilled my expectations," he notes, " and I think there is more to explore. Just like the show itself, once you open a doorway into a character's past, a dozen more show up in front of you. But I'm interested in knowing what happened to Michael during those years between the day he has to say goodbye to Walt and the day he saw him return.

JOSH'S NEW MOVIE

Forthcoming feature film *Whisper* sees JOSH HOLLOWAY once again coming into conflict with the law and those things that go bump in the night...

"I play Max in *Whisper*," he explains. "Max has fallen in love and wants to make a better life for himself and his fiancée. However, due to his criminal past, he's unable to accomplish that. He tries the old 'do this one last job' to get them on their feet. They kidnap a child for ransom and as it turns out, the kid is more than what they had bargained for. He's not just a "normal" kid and that is when all the creepy stuff starts happening. As an actor, what I found interesting about Max is that he is motivated by love and desperation to do a very bad thing. I liked the irony."

"Between the time he let go of his son and saw him again, who was Michael and how does that part translate into his character now? I am interested in what the other sides of Michael will be. I am already prodding the writers and plotting ideas. Nobody is all good or bad. Michael is probably a bit of an asshole himself with a determined 'I am going to make this happen' attitude that lends to big mistakes."

At one point, Locke tells Shannon the island is their opportunity to restart their lives, for redemption. Michael has certainly grabbed that second chance when it comes to Walt but what about Sawyer? Can a leopard truly change its spots? "It absolutely applies to Sawyer and his journey," states Holloway. "He's learned to survive by using his anger and the island is forcing him to face the reason behind it."

Sawyer has more to deal with than anger management. Despite protests, his crude jokes and lustful stares have ignited a spark between him and Kate but then again, Jack also seems to have his eye on the beautiful fugitive. "Jack is a compassionate good guy who represents more how men are expected to be today," offers Holloway. "Sawyer is more like how men used to be before they were forced to be politically correct. And Kate is attracted to both types and the struggle to decide is interesting to watch."

Things further heat up between Kate and Sawyer during a boar hunt in *Outlaws* when they play a personal tell-all drinking game. The Sawyer heavy chapter showcases his tormented existence by revealing that as a child, he was present for his Mom's murder and Dad's suicide. Seeking vengeance 20 years later against the man Sawyer blames for their death, he travels to Australia and kills the man he believes was responsible. However, Sawyer soon discovers he was set up to kill an innocent man. "We both had a good time shooting that episode and it was one of our favorite scenes together so far," says Holloway of the campfire confessions.

"Sawyer handles his wound in the classical Sawyer way — with defiance and denial. Underneath, he's truly afraid and doesn't want to die."
— *Josh Holloway*

"Why hasn't Sawyer gotten any action?!"

— Josh Holloway

On the flip side, *Confidence Man* proved to be a painfully taxing experience when Sawyer is sadistically tortured by Jack and Sayid for the location of Shannon's inhalers. "I spent two 14 hour days on my knees with my hands tied with a cord," recalls Holloway. "It was certainly physically demanding and emotionally draining. That type of intense scene is always challenging and fun to do as an actor."

Perrineau had his own experience with an intense scene when he unintentionally ruffles Jin's feathers which results in the Korean beating the crap out of him and nearly drowning him. Although it boiled down to a matter of honor, Perrineau initially had reservations about the incident. "At first, I was a little concerned because of my normal relationship with television and the way they tell stories with people," explains Perrineau. "My concern was 'Oh, they are going to have the people of color kicking each other's butts all the time.' Often when you have a black character, every time they tell a story, it is about him being black as if that is all there is. So I was concerned the minorities were kicking each other's ass again because that is what they do. I was really happy we didn't go that route and that we made both of these guys multi-dimensional and out of this heavy strife of language and cultural communication gap, that they have somehow formed this interesting bond."

Arguably, no one wants off the damn island more than Michael and it is that determination which leads him to build a raft. When his first attempt is burned to a crisp, suspicions fall on Jin. Later when Michael is poisoned from spiked water, the finger is pointed at Sawyer. Portraying that sudden illness proved to be one of Perrineau's greatest challenges on *Lost*. "This may sound odd but the toughest scene I've done is where Michael gets sick," reveals Perrineau. "You would think having a stomach ache would be really easy, but there is so much more involved in that to pull it off credibly, making me more insecure than anything. You have to feel the sting that is not at all happening to you so technically things like when Michael gets hurt or has a limp, those are the hardest to pull off. The other stuff isn't as hard, physically speaking. Just emotionally tough."

Ironically enough, when the raft sets sail, Michael finds himself with Walt and two unlikely candidates: Jin and Sawyer. "Those choices were interesting because at the end of the day, they are all still stuck on the island and desperately still need to get off for whatever reason," offers Perrineau. "Building a raft created a situation that changes a negative to a positive. Jin's subbornness might not normally be an asset, but in this case it was. And Sawyer may be smarmy, but without his stash the raft could never have been completed. Jack has the worries of the entire community there, Locke is worried about the island, Claire has her baby… These three are just worried about getting the hell out of there."

In the season one finale, not only is the hatch finally opened but the true nailbiter sees Michael, Jin, Sawyer, and Walt finally shipping off on their raft in search of help. However, on the open water, everything goes wrong. After desperately firing a flare gun to attract attention, they stumbled across a small tugboat helmed by the sinister Others who all in the blink of an eye kidnapped Walt, shot Sawyer, blew up the raft, and left Michael treading water alone. "I loved it!" raves Holloway about the two hour *Exodus*. "It was dynamic, intense, and one heck of a cliffhanger."

As usual, it teased as much as it resolved. "I was wondering where this was going to go and how it was going to play out," reflects Perrineau. "And being a non swimmer, at the time, I believed Michael was dead," he laughs. "This is it. Nice year. But it has taken an interesting turn and the finale was actually the beginning of this huge adventure."

Ah yes. With Jin missing, Sawyer and Michael bickered as they floated on the remains of the raft. As they continued to argue, they encountered a shark with a distinct marking on its tail. Spending days on the ocean shooting, Holloway notes that, "All the water scenes are both physically and emotionally challenging. Thank God I don't get seasick."

Eventually, Michael and Sawyer washed up on shore where they joined Jin in captivity of the 'Tallies.' Thrown into a pit, crisis mode kicked in. For Sawyer, who is mortally wounded and needs medical attention, that predictably means being uncooperative. "Sawyer handles his wound in the classical Sawyer way – with defiance and denial," says Holloway. "Underneath, he's truly afraid and doesn't want to die. As far as how it affects his way of thinking when he makes it back to the camp, we'll just have to wait and see."

Michael, who blames himself for taking Walt on the raft in the first place, "is having to quell his emotions in order to think clearly enough to get the job done," reveals Perrineau. "At the end of the day, he has to figure out what to do to get Walt back. He has outbursts and I think it's actually going to drive him crazy. He still believes his son could be somewhere on the water – he is forced to consider that possibility. Michael doesn't know anything about the Others. I have to find as much information as I can but I could flip and get killed. He is handling it as well as he can."

Perrineau points out their predicament will shed a new light on Michael, Sawyer, and Jin. "You'll see their relationship go through a lot of changes through contempt to possibly friends," he says. "Thanks to the 'Tailies,' they are oddly joined at the hip."

Besides tangling with a polar bear, Michael has been insulated from all the island's strange going-ons, so naturally Perrineau is excited about how the current storyline is sucking him into that weirdness. "Yeah, I am," he confirms. "We are adding the adventure part that some other characters had last season. It is really cool. I like the action and there are so many dilemmas going on at one time."

Obviously, Perrineau and Holloway can't spill any of the upcoming twists and turns but hint the trio will be learning more about the 'Tailies' people. "They are really skittish and the question Michael has is 'Why?'" muses Perrineau. "There's a 'monster' out there, but they are acting bizarre. Clearly, it is safer on our side of the island, so we are heading back there. I think the 'Tailies' are looking for someone to take them there, but Michael is still consumed with Walt and he will manipulate people to try and get his son back."

No doubt fans are eagerly anticipating Sawyer and Kate locking lips again but will his absence truly have made their hearts grow fonder? "I don't know how reuniting with Kate will strengthen or weaken their relationship," reports Holloway. "It is yet to be discovered. However, their current relationship definitely is motivating his will to survive."

This season has witnessed some new additions to the cast including Adewale Akinnuoye-Agbaje, Cynthia Watros and Michelle Rodriguez and Holloway is pleased with the change in dynamic. "I feel like it's added another dimension to the show," he says. "The writers are brilliant and they never cease to amaze me. Also, it has been a pleasure working with the new cast members. I feel like they are definitely bringing something to the show."

Since tuning in, *Lost* fans have discussed and debated theories but they aren't the only ones banging their heads. One of the big secrets is also driving Perrineau nuts. "The next storyline will answer more questions but then you go 'How does that work?' says Perrineau. "I really want to know the deal about the Others. I'm really confused about them. Who they are? And remember Ethan? What was that about?"

As for Holloway, there's only one thing that has been bothering him "Why hasn't Sawyer gotten any action?!" he deadpans.

LOST ON TRACK

Why HAROLD PERRINEAU believes the show gets it "just right"…

When the innovative *The Matrix* downloaded into theatres, anticipation was so high for the sequels that it was hard living up to the hype and moviegoers were disappointed. Harold Perrineau, who co-starred in those second installments, realized season two of *Lost* could have easily suffered a similar frustrating fate.

"Yeah, there was a big concern not only on my part but everybody's part," he says. "One, the sophomore curse and two, the writers

make it look easy but I know it is not. There are a lot of stories that can be told and a lot of ways to go. It could easily be Land of the *Lost*, dinosaurs, the cheesiest thing you've ever seen or it could keep being great. With a show that inspires this level of passion, we are always riding an ultra-thin line between not enough and too much. As each script is received there is a feeling of, 'Is this going to hold up?' but it always does. It's a real blessing. We all just have to keep working."

LOST

FALLING FROM GRACE

Sayid and Shannon have shared several emotional experiences together, from the death of Boone, to the revelation of their love for each other. NAVEEN ANDREWS and MAGGIE GRACE discuss the warmth of their characters' feelings for one another, and the cold, harsh realities of the island...

For all the great mysteries of the *Lost* island (i.e. 'monsters,' polar bears and the Others), there are just as many subtle enigmas simmering and shaping the unfolding events of the story. For instance, just look at the diverse mix of survivors alone, which includes a doctor and a felon, a scoundrel and a lottery winner, even an ex-Republican Iraqi Guard and a spoiled brat with a huge chip on her shoulder. How they connect in their new environment is the core of what makes *Lost* so compelling, with the unexpected connections and alliances between supposed equals or opposites making the drama so profound. Of all the relationships on the show, one of the least expected is that of the romantic connection between the soulful Iraqi, Sayid, and the petulant young woman, Shannon.

While on the surface, this passionate match may have always seemed at odds with the character's true natures, the island and the *Lost* producers know that transforming the expected into the unexpected is always the path to truth and revelation. The same applies to the actors playing the lovers, veteran British actor and Emmy nominee Naveen Andrews, and the American newcomer, Maggie Grace. With a 14-year age difference, and completely different personal and professional backgrounds, the actors are seemingly as opposite as their characters, but in reality, like their onscreen counterparts, they are truly kindred spirits on other levels, such as how they approach their craft, the challenges of shooting the show and their mutual respect for one another as friends and colleagues. Sayid and Shannon's slow evolution from friends to lovers over the last year ended with a brutal climax in the episode *Abandoned*, which hailed the death of Shannon and their newly consummated relationship. The pair recently talked to *Lost Magazine* about working together on the series, the repercussions of Shannon's demise and how the show has changed their lives forever...

London-born Andrews, best known for his work on the stage and in films *The English Patient* and *Karma Sutra*, admits when the script for the pilot for *Lost* crossed his path, he was perplexed immediately by the challenges it offered. "I would presume most actors would fear when they are given a script that doesn't have a beginning middle, or an end," he laughs. "In film, you know what your character is and the part you are going to play and hopefully, you have an arc and an ending. With *Lost*, it is constantly evolving and you literally don't know what is happening, so you find you make certain choices early on about character and you hope they are the right ones."

Landing the role of Sayid Jarrah, an ex-Republican Iraqi soldier with a tragic past, the actor says the character was one of the most unique ever offered to him. "I suppose the thing that first attracted me to the character was that he was the least like who he said he was. He served in the Republican Guard and was an Iraqi. To have that on primetime TV was shocking in itself! It was the first thing that intrigued me and I still can't believe it now, considering the political climate we live in at the moment."

Discussing his approach in developing Sayid, Andrews details, "Once I started establishing the character, I thought it was pretty important to bring in certain elements that, at least on the surface, don't have anything to do with his profile. At the same time, there's an aesthetic about him and a certain calmness that is also valuable in a situation when most people are in a total panic. Apart from that, I wanted to introduce a kind of romantic side to him and that was apparent from the pilot and it's grown with his back-story and his relationship with Shannon."

For Maggie Grace, getting the role of Shannon was an important step in her young career. "When I first read for Shannon, there were the basic bones of the character." In other words, Shannon's angry disposition and disdain for her brother Boone (Ian Somerhalder) and the rest of the crash survivors. The character immediately became a lightning rod for audience dislike, which was perfect for Grace.

NAVEEN'S NOMINATION

The actor behind Sayid Jarrah talks about his recent Emmy nomination for Supporting Actor in a Drama Series...

"It's very nice to get some kind of acknowledgment for your work," said Andrews. Although this marked the actor's first-ever Emmy nomination he said, "It's bloody good for the show. We're all pretty proud of it. It's a great thing to be involved in."

Andrews paid tribute to fellow nominee (in the same category) and co-star Terry O'Quinn, saying, "I really admire him as an actor. To be in the same category as him is a true honor."

LOCKE & LOAD

NAVEEN ANDREWS and **MAGGIE GRACE** on why Locke rocks their world...

MG: Oh, Locke. I love the way Terry approaches him and it's really amazing to watch. He's an incredibly, exquisitely experienced actor and it's really cool what he's done with Locke. There's so many surprising elements to him that no one saw coming, from the moment we realized he was in a wheelchair before the crash, to when his father said he's not wanted and how that hit him. It's been a pleasure to watch.

NA: Terry brings a weight to that character like King Lear. It requires a lot and it's one of the most intriguing characters I've ever seen on TV. Terry brings an element of mystery and a deep sense of ambivalence. You don't know which way he is coming from or where he is going to go.

> "...Our past before the plane crash is somehow no longer relevant to these surroundings. In a way, it's your soul that is brought out without the formalities and bullshit, basically, of so-called civilized living!"
>
> — Naveen Andrews

"I embraced that controversial aspect of her and it was really fun. I had played sweet, innocent, naïve girl-next-doors for five years, so it was a nice change to play a character with more layers. I'm glad that not every character was sympathetic at first on *Lost*. They are on an island, so you have to build some conflict and have your characters serve the show as much as possible. If that means, perhaps starting out a bit more two-dimensional and with a few more unsympathetic qualities at first, so be it," she says candidly.

Yet both actors admit, one of the greatest challenges of *Lost* is coming to terms with never knowing the full history about their characters. "I've taken a huge stab at creating a back-story and trying to have that inform my work as much as possible, but, at the end of the day I just have to hope I'm not off-base," says Grace. "Sometimes in light of things you discover later you learn there might be ways of doing it a bit differently. Even though it's an additional challenge, I like to do as much research as possible, building as specific a history as possible. I usually fill notebooks with work, but it's difficult to be terribly sure of yourself here, so you have to jump and hope the net is there for you. It's a different way of working, but I appreciate that and I have a lot of trust in Damon and J.J. in seeing this through. Again, the choices are made on what's best for the show. What's best is keeping that aloof quality and to keep it open. They do change plans sometimes and storylines and have these amazing revelatory ideas and so they'll add and change things. I think we've all had the rug pulled out from under us quite a few times, but there's no resentment there. We all understand the situation."

Andrews concurs adding, "I think the hardest thing is to try to keep yourself in a state of openness and readiness for whatever might happen. To not become too fixed or precious about things that you might consider to be part of your character, because you might have to adjust. It's important to stay open to that. It's a new thing for me to play a character over this long a period of time. The longest I've done it for a film was four months. Trying to sustain a character over a period of time and still come up with stuff you feel is fresh and interesting and at the same time being true to the character is hard."

Andrews adds that it's also hard being as calm and collected as Sayid is. "What's completely foreign to me is his technical ability. I can barely change a light bulb! I'm useless and I wouldn't be able to cope in that situation at all. Even now, changing the strings on my guitar is a major operation to undertake. His kind of groundedness and that particular kind of calm during extreme stress is foreign to me too," he chuckles.

Reflecting on the first season, Grace says in lieu of not getting her own flashback episode, she ranks the revelation of her sleeping with her stepbrother Boone in his episode as a huge moment for her character. "I knew there was more to the story and I kind of suspected it earlier just based on a couple things in the writing and a couple strange comments from Damon that made me go, 'Wait a minute!'" she laughs. "It was an interesting way to go. It was fun and I was really happy they made her have qualities like that. It's all about her surviving, both on the island and in the world before the crash. She did what was necessary and it was great to see more of her in that way and less surface bickering. There was a lot more to it than just slamming Boone, but that was fun too!"

Andrews cites his own highlights saying, "Apart from how elated I was with the way the writers established the Sayid character and have been able to write for him, [my highlight] was an isolated moment. I was reading a Locke episode and sifting through it and there was a point where he crawls over to the hatch and says, 'I can't do anymore. You have to give me a sign.' It's almost biblical and he's crying and a light comes on. It was small, but for me it was huge! I leapt up screaming and shouting when I read it saying, "These people are wild!' It was totally unexpected. To be able to do that, because when I first read the pilot about a plane crash on an island, I thought it was boring! How long could they go on with that? But Damon has these constant permutations of different situations."

"The choices are made on what's best for the show. I think we've all had the rug pulled out from under us quite a few times, but there's no resentment there. We all understand the situation."

Maggie Grace

Executive Producer Jack Bender takes five with Naveen Andrews

50

"I like the fact that the relationship with Shannon came from left field and there was no way that you could predict it."

— Naveen Andrews

One of those permutations included the romance between Sayid and Shannon. While her arc may have been less ornate compared to some other characters, Shannon really began to blossom in her growing relationship with Sayid. Although, at first, many believed that Shannon was just playing with Sayid, Grace says she never questioned it was real for her character. "I certainly felt that was a very truthful relationship and there was real vulnerability there. I didn't think that was another one of her manipulations. I was really happy to see more of her character come out in that relationship. Plus, I get to work with Naveen because of it," she says.

Andrews says their developing relationship was oddly perfect for the show. "I like the fact that the relationship with Shannon came from left field and there was no way that you could predict it. I like the fact that you can't chart how it could have happened. I like to think part of it is situation – being on an island and being male and female. And then there is the idea that our past before the plane crash is somehow no longer relevant in these surroundings. In a way, it's your soul that is brought out without the formalities and the bullshit, basically, of so-called civilized living."

Grace agrees and offers, "There were a couple of scenes where she gradually began to trust Sayid more and she comes to realize that who she is isn't sufficient. It's sort of a rebirth, which is a theme for our show – the idea and the opportunity to begin anew, because the island is the great leveler. It's just a lot more literal on our show."

Returning for season two, both actors admit that the immense media attention and Emmy wins have changed the dynamic on the show and in their own lives. "To be honest, a lot changed. I don't think it's productive to view it as positive or negative. Really, it's just inevitable," Grace offers. "It's honestly a wonderful situation. I think the writers are a great group and we still look forward to what we are getting from them each week. We are all very invested in what we are doing." Andrews adds, "The whole experience in every way has been an education, of sorts. The publicity this thing has attracted and the way it has changed, for better or for worse, all of our lives. It's a nice dilemma to have, but it introduces a whole new set of problems. You have to grow up and be an adult about it, whatever that means," he smiles.

Fortunately, the actors say the work for season two has been just as engaging and rewarding especially with the deepening of their characters' relationship. "We work very well together, at least from my point of view," Grace smiles. "It was great to have someone that wants to rehearse. He's so open to work off of and is so giving. It's important to trust someone like that especially with the things we have been doing recently emotionally, it's a really beautiful thing to look in someone's eyes and feel safe and he's been there for me. I think it's made me a better actor in so many ways. It's been a real gift."

Andrews is equally complimentary, "I think she is streets ahead in terms of dealing with this business than I was at her age. I greatly admire that and I think she has a very special quality of giving her character a new depth and maturity that wasn't there before. You are seeing a young woman come forth and in an almost surprising original sort of innocence."

LOST TOGETHER

NAVEEN ANDREWS and **MAGGIE GRACE** discuss how they felt when the large cast was assembled…

MG: It was so nerve-wracking meeting everyone. A lot was riding on that because you don't know how long the experience will go on. It could be six weeks or six years, so I was nervous to meet everyone, but they exceeded my highest hopes. It's an amazing group of people and it's amazing how closely we've bonded. My closest friends are on this show and I feel they will remain so even after, even when the show is no longer.

We are so different and at different stages in our lives. I turned 21 on this show and I'm in a different place in my life than most cast members, but it was amazing how much common ground we did find. And how many sunrises I've watched with these people and how many debates we've gotten into in the small hours! I couldn't ask for a better group. I know people always say it's a great family, but this was right on, right away. I've never been part of something like this before, such camaraderie in a group and it's been beautiful for me.

NA: One of the surprises is that we got such a good group of people. We all get on and we kind of look out for each other too. We knew right from the beginning if this thing took off, we would be stuck with one another whether we liked it or not. It's like a family. Ultimately, we all care about the work and we want to do as good a job as possible. In order to facilitate that, it's important we don't hate one another [laughs].

Sadly, Shannon's journey follows that of her doomed brother and his demise in season one. While audiences may have been shocked at her violent death at the hands of tail-section survivor Ana Lucia (Michele Rodriguez), Grace says she knew her end was coming. "I'm not terribly conflicted about it," she says candidly. "Overall, I knew what was going to happen. I knew for quite some time and it wasn't a shock to get the script. They are much more sensitive and wonderful than that. They are respectful of the fact that we have lives [in Hawaii] and some people have kids in school. They try to do it in the best way possible, but it's something we have been aware of from day one. So when you get the call, it's not a shock like you might get on another show. I think it was sort of obvious in the writing in how they didn't really develop the character [a lot]. I think that indicated where they were heading, so it's not something I was completely taken aback by, even if I thought it might happen later. If it's going to be unexpected, it's more beautiful that way. Even if I had the shorter straw of the bunch, as far as time, it's still an amazing bunch of straws."

Grace details the knowledge of her death was tempered with the fact that she finally got a back-story episode that revealed why Shannon has become so bitter about her family and life in general. It was a huge window into her character's soul and a gratifying answer to why her character was so troubled. "The only value in my coming back for a second season was if we developed the character. There was no point offing some sacrificial lamb. You have to care about the character to give the situation any impact at all. What's important about ending this character is how it can help the show. It needs to provoke as much as possible to give other characters a chance to develop their relationship a little more. I think there were some really beautiful moments in the script. A lot of it was new and a lot wasn't, in terms of how I was dying. It was certainly a challenge to [go to] work at the last minute and get a script the day before where you are in most the scenes. I was certainly helped by great writing."

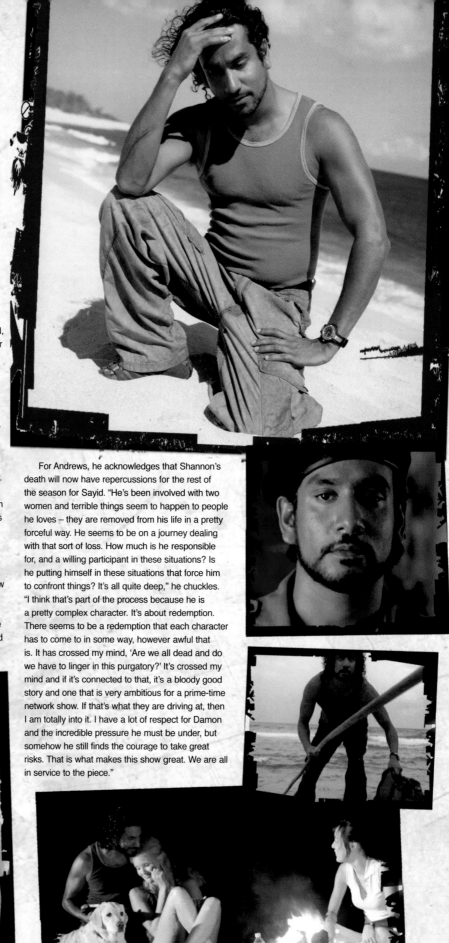

For Andrews, he acknowledges that Shannon's death will now have repercussions for the rest of the season for Sayid. "He's been involved with two women and terrible things seem to happen to people he loves – they are removed from his life in a pretty forceful way. He seems to be on a journey dealing with that sort of loss. How much is he responsible for, and a willing participant in these situations? Is he putting himself in these situations that force him to confront things? It's all quite deep," he chuckles. "I think that's part of the process because he is a pretty complex character. It's about redemption. There seems to be a redemption that each character has to come to in some way, however awful that is. It has crossed my mind, 'Are we all dead and do we have to linger in this purgatory?' It's crossed my mind and if it's connected to that, it's a bloody good story and one that is very ambitious for a prime-time network show. If that's what they are driving at, then I am totally into it. I have a lot of respect for Damon and the incredible pressure he must be under, but somehow he still finds the courage to take great risks. That is what makes this show great. We are all in service to the piece."

THE WATCHERS

NAVEEN ANDREWS and **MAGGIE GRACE** discuss viewing their performances in the final cut episodes...

NA: To be really honest, I am always very self-critical. I don't actually watch the show. It's probably a personal problem – I could do it when I was younger, but I made a false wall to protect me. Now, having to watch myself is really distressing. I can enjoy everyone else's performances, but as soon as I come on, the whole thing is ruined, so I figure why put myself through it [laughs]?
MG: I know Naveen has a hard time watching his work and I can identify with that. There are always small choices in light of the bigger stories that I would change.

> "Personally, I've grown up a lot on the show. I've learned so much and I don't mean just as far as the work. It's helped me out a lot."
>
> — Maggie Grace

Remembering her last day on the set, Grace is upbeat and actually grateful, despite the sadness of the event. "My last day I thought would be bittersweet, but it ended up being really fun. It was like graduation where everyone signs your yearbook. I have so many pictures from that day with the crew and certain people that I've really come to know and love. We have a truly exceptional crew. There are long hours and the lack of sleep is unbelievable. Sometimes we have three units running at the same time and they work so hard and the actors tend to get most of the credit because we are the front men, but they work their butts off!"

While the actors say they will miss working with one another immensely, they are both appreciative of what the show has given them so far and what they both know it will continue to give them long into the future. Grace closes with conviction, "Personally and professionally, it's been amazing. I've never been a part of something like this on so many levels or something so successful. On a professional level, it's opened so many doors for all of us. Personally, I've grown up a lot on the show. I've learned so much and I don't mean just as far as the work. It's helped me out a lot." Andrews smiles, and offers, "We have to deliver a good show and I really believe that you can do things in television that you can't do on film. To that extent, it's an art form and if we can approach doing a good piece of art now and again, I'm happy."

SAIL AWAY

It's well and truly lost at sea, but before our heroes' raft was blown to pieces, it played an important part in the survivors' story. Designer **RON YATES** talks exclusively about making the vessel out of salvaged plane wreckage and bamboo…

How did you find yourself landing your role on *Lost*?
The main producers hire heads of departments who then crew up [themselves] down the line. I was hired by Carlos Barbosa who wasn't the Production Designer on the pilot but was on the first 11 episodes of last season. After he left, Stephen Storer and Mimi Gramicci came in for the last half and they inherited me [laughs].

Did the creative team divulge how pivotal the raft would be?
The writers were not very forthcoming as to how many people it would have to support so in terms of its size, it was left up to us.

It is kind of policy on *Lost*. They are very cagey about details. When we did the hatch, we had no idea what was below there.

When they asked you to do the raft, what kind of specifications did they give you?
As far as building the raft, what was required on the beach was that 'in progress' raft. We were also busy doing the actual one that would be used on the ocean. So there are two [being made] simultaneously. Then after the fire, one was rebuilt. Once the raft itself was seaworthy, they wanted an additional half-version that would be floating on a barge so it would be easier to shoot, [but] the original raft worked so well, the half-version wasn't needed.

Did you use a template for the raft?
Stephen, the Production Designer, didn't want to go with the usual castaway 'Huck Finn' sort of raft. He wanted something more interesting. He was inspired by the Polynesian Catamaran design which has been in use for centuries.

Our survivors were left with a challenge in terms of how to construct a raft from the vegetation and debris from the crash that made it to the beach. We used that set of circumstances as a place to start.

As far as the design goes, the concept was a collaboration between Stephen and myself. We developed the look and it went through a series of changes. Once we had approval of what the raft would look like, the characters began 'making' theirs over a series of episodes.

WINDS OF CHANGE

For fans hungry for raft diary information, RON YATES notes the various stages of its life on the show…

"Well, if you look at the timeline from the story point of view:

Day 28: Michael decides to build the raft to get him and Walt off the island.

Day 33: Walt burns the raft and Michael suspects Jin.

Day 35: They start rebuilding the new raft.

Day 43: Arzt warns them of the changes of the winds and that they need to sail immediately.

Day 44: The rudder and the mast gets damaged which holds things up for several hours. By night of day 44, they've set sail and the raft is blown up."

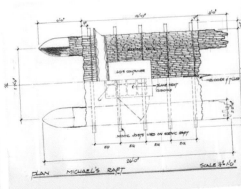

"Three months prior {to the raft's launch}, huge waves were coming in so our sets on the beach had to be moved. But the gods were really smiling on us the day of the launch and the ocean was flat."

CAPTAIN JIM

RON YATES is the first to give credit where credit is due – when it comes to the raft sinking or floating, he gives top props to Jim Van Houton...

"The man that is truly responsible for the success in terms of its seaworthiness, making the mast collapse, working out the rudder, and figuring out the displacement in the water was Jim. He is our all around genius sculptor and without him, we'd literally be lost. He even sculpted the whole Black Rock ship – the show is so dependent on him."

Obviously, the real raft isn't made of trees, rope, and crazy glue. Can you detail the process of erecting it?

My version of the one actually built was a sub-structure which was then laminated with bamboo and covered over to look like the one being built on the beach.

Jim Van Houton built three little models of that super-structure to make it strong enough. With the waters around here in Hawaii, it had to be rigid. The idea that we came up with was to have two 20-foot long, 28-inch diameter culvert pipes, which were later filled with foam. Each one of them had four metal straps bound around them. This was attached to a tubular sub-deck which straddled the two pontoons which was welded together by Alan Kiriu.

Jim's team skimmed down the whole thing with bamboo to make it look like the one on the beach.

Stephen introduced the idea of using an air container, and Jim sort of scaled it down so it didn't take up too much deck space. The sail was apparently supposed to come from the remnants of the escape chute from the plane which was umbrella fabric.

Originally, we thought it would have to be towed. Usually your rudders are behind each pontoon, but I realized Michael wouldn't have the sophistication of a tiller, so we set it in the center.

I ordered an overall bin from a company in Hollywood that supplies airplane parts, so we attached that to the back of the container to put supplies in.

There were a few prototypes discussed. What was the biggest challenge in perfecting it?

The biggest challenge was to have it seaworthy enough to support a camera crew, the actors, and for it to be safe. The prop on the beach was a bundle of bamboo tied together with wire [laughs]!

There is a scene where the cast is pushing and shoving the raft towards the water. How heavy was it?

It is an extremely heavy raft. We laid out logs very similar to building the pyramids. We also created a track it could run along.

Part of the gag is the raft slides off those and you have to lever it back on. That was pretty complicated. Initially, we were told it would never launch from the beach so we weren't really prepared for that kind of set-up..

When the raft hits the ocean, did it float on its inaugural voyage out?

Oh yes. It was interesting to see because this crane camera came in. There is a canal that flows right next to the construction mill so it was simply a question of lifting it up, pivoting it around, and lowering it down. It floated perfectly. Once we added bamboo, it gave it extra displacement.

During production, how vulnerable was the raft to the whims of Mother Nature?

In December of last year, they held the Eddie Aikau Invitational. When waves reach 20-feet at Waimea Bay in Hawaii, they have a surfing competition. The bay is only three and a half miles from where the raft was launched. Three months prior, huge waves were coming in so most of our sets on the beach had to be moved back. But the gods were really smiling on us the day of the launch and the ocean was flat.

THE OTHERS

Executive Producer **CARLTON CUSE** looks back on how he became part of the *LOST* team and discusses his role on the show...

Let's start with a *Lost* style flashback. What is *your* flashback – the events that led you to you being *Lost*?

I knew Damon [Lindelof] because I gave Damon his first staff job on a show that I created called *Nash Bridges*. Damon was an incredibly talented young writer on that show, and we became not only colleagues, but friends. As Damon began working on *Lost*, we would just talk as friends. He was telling me about the show, and keeping me up to speed with what was going on. He sent me the pilot [episode] to look at, and I absolutely loved it. It was brilliant – he and J.J. had done an amazing job. [Damon and J.J.] actually turned what wasn't the greatest idea for a TV show into something quite brilliant.

I got hooked on the show, but in the meantime I had a development deal with Sony Television. As time went on, and the first few episodes of *Lost* had aired, it became apparent to Damon that he needed some help running the show. His role has many facets. It's not just about coming up with the episodes each week – which is hard enough [laughs] – its also about managing a company that employs 225 people – it's a giant enterprise. So, Damon asked me if I would be interested in coming over and working on the show.

I met with him and J.J. [Abrams] and [originally] wasn't particularly interested in going to work on somebody else's show, but I fell in love with *Lost* and in love with the material. That's what drew me in and I said, "Yes." It's a fantastic piece of work, and I felt that I could bring something to it. That was the combination of things that led me here.

"WE CAN HAVE SOMEONE BEING TORTURED, AND IN THE SOMEONE

"Season two is going to be about the fact that they realize they may be stuck here for a while. That changes them."

At which point did you officially join Team *Lost*?

I started getting involved in the storymaking process as we moved towards the middle of the season. It was not my intention to reinvent the wheel, it was really just about trying to help out the workload and embellish the work that had already been done. There was so much mythological framework that J.J. and Damon had created, I just added some pieces and elements to that. I don't really like to dissect that – in some ways it takes something away from the magic of the final shows. The process is putting all those elements together, to make the final episodes better than the sum of their parts.

Most importantly I think that Damon and I discovered quite quickly that we had a real aesthetics similarity, and bond. We thought of the show in the same way and in the same terms. The value of having a collaborator and someone to bounce those ideas off of is really helpful and important when you're actually trying to turn out a script literally every eight shooting days. The challenge and the pressure of network television is you try to make the episodes really good, but you're doing that against this constantly ticking clock. You have a finite amount of time in which to make each one of these episodes good.

SAME EPISODE, PLAYING GOLF . . ."

57

"I think the hatch is sort of a literal metaphor — for going inward and going inside."

Director Jack Bender discusses Evangeline Lilly's next scene for the season two opener *Man of Science, Man of Faith*

13D

LOST

J. BENDER   EP#201

M. BONVILLAIN A.S.C.

KALEIDOSCOPE

CARLTON CUSE addresses the huge variety of storytelling styles that *Lost* has become so well known for...

"The season one Hurley episode [*Numbers*] was very consciously written as a black comedy. Other episodes can be like the Locke-centric episodes – pretty mystical and very much centered around the weird mythology of this hatch, whilst others can be very straight, character-orientated and not have much in the way of mythological elements. I love the fact that we can engage in those different types of storytelling."

> "It's a little bit like being an air traffic controller. The episodes are like the planes that you're trying to guide into a safe landing, but at the same time you're still trying to manage the seven other planes that have their own flight patterns."

Which flavors/tones of *Lost* appeal to you the most?

What makes *Lost* more than just another genre show is the intense focus on the characters and especially the characters' back-stories. The flashback device – which is a brilliant creation that allowed the show to expand – that's the essence of why 20 million people watch the show every week. They're very drawn to these characters, as was I, and as I continue to be. Working on the show every day, I'm learning more about the characters as we talk about them in the Writers' Room. As we chart their future stories – based on what we know about them and what is special about them – they become self-contained stories within the episodes that reveal a lot about who these people are.

I think that all of us have seminal moments in our lives. If you sat down and had a drink with somebody, began talking, and became friends, you would probably uncover five or six things in their lives that help define them as the person they are. What we're doing on the show is showing the audience those events, some of which have been shared with other characters. What's interesting about the show is that we as an audience know more about the interior lives of our characters than their fellow characters do. That's something that also makes the show different from other shows.

I have a lot of background doing action adventure – the movie-like qualities of the series. The 'man versus nature' elements, I love all that stuff and I feel very at home with that, too. I love the fact that it's not just a procedural type of genre show. It's not in a box – it's a show that has a lot of room to let us do lots of different types of story. We can have someone being tortured, and in the same episode, someone playing a round of golf. That latitude is what makes the show fun to write.

And what would be a typical 'day in the life of Carlton Cuse on *Lost*'?

Usually a typical day starts with Damon and I having breakfast together, sitting right here in my office, or in the delicious and wonderful Disney commissary [laughs]. We usually talk about what the issues of the day are. Those range from the practical issues involved with production and managing of the show, to the creative direction, and ideas that we've had about where the show should go. Or, we might go over a specific story. There isn't really a typical day for me. Any given day can be focused on many different things. Some quieter days I might be in the Writers' Room, on other days I might be on the phone with production issues. I also might be doing production rewrites, having a 'tone meeting' with the directors to establish what the intent is of a script, or dealing with publicity. There are so many different aspects to the job.

At any given time, six to eight shows are in various stages of the process – from the first initial concept phase, to the script outline, pre-production, one will be shooting, several are in post-production. It's a little bit like being an air traffic controller. The episodes are like the planes that you're trying to guide into a safe landing, but at the same time you're still trying to manage the seven other planes that have their own flight patterns. The 'spinning plates' is another good metaphor. There's always something going on. It's like having a term paper in college every eight days, but there is a wonderful energy in that, which I've always loved. It's something that I enjoy the pressure of, working under those circumstances.

The finale of the first season ended up being an epic three hours – how did that come about?

As we started working out the story, it became apparent that we had enough story to fill three hours in order to tell this adventure. As Damon, the writers and I all worked out the [finale's] stories, it became apparent that this season's ending was an opportunity to bring a sense of closure and completion to the whole first year of the show. One of the things we were really conscious about doing was trying to answer a bunch of mysteries, unlike *Twin Peaks* or *The X-Files* – there was a lot of mythology [in those shows] but it was frustrating because things were raised and then never answered. We had a list on the white boards in the Writers' Room of some of *Lost*'s mysteries, and we were ticking off the ones we felt we could successfully answer in this finale. While not answering the larger questions like, 'What was the island?' we all felt we gave the audience more information about the 'monster', visually, the nature of the island, and we could explain some things like, 'What is The Black Rock?' So we filled out certain things and brought closure to some of the things that were issues for the first season.

We had this idea of giving each of the characters a flashback [in the finale]. Showing the day of the flight showed how these characters that we've come to know got on the plane. Having that as the end of the first season worked well with where the whole series started.

Any favored mysteries of the island?

I was compelled by the hatch, when I first heard about it. I thought Locke's connection to the hatch, and the fact that Locke puts all his spiritual weight on it – that he believes that opening the hatch is going to provide him with the answers about this island – was really compelling. I love the hatch.

I've also been very engaged by the 'monster' and the decision to show a little more of the 'monster' was something I felt strongly about. I feel like while we will continue to tease out the answers as to what the 'monster' is, we're making forward progress – we're not just treating it the same every time.

How does this new season differ from the first year?

We're going to try and make season two have a distinctly different feel to it than season one. We'll still have all the same elements – flashbacks, etc, and we're not going to radically overhaul the show – but I think what we're going to try to create is a sense that episodes can kind of stand on their own. We feel like there's a completed arc for season one.

The first season was really about these people being in denial over their fate. They were on this island and they were expecting to be rescued, but when they aren't immediately rescued, they build a raft – their plan is to get off this island, get help and get the hell out of there.

Season two is going to be about the fact that they realize they may be stuck here for a while. That changes them, and forces them to turn a little bit more inward. I think the hatch is sort of a literal metaphor: for going inward and going inside. They're going to be doing a little bit more society building and also exploring the island too. △

> *"I feel like while we will continue to tease out the answers as to what the 'monster' is, we're making forward progress – we're not just treating it the same every time..."*

THE PRESIDENT SPEAKS

From a standard end-of-season finale to an epic three-hour event, CARLTON CUSE reveals how the ABC President's phone calls evolved *Exodus*…

"Originally, Stephen McPherson, the President of ABC, called us and asked us whether we could do an extra hour of the show, and we agreed. Then he called again and asked if we could do a *second* extra hour of the show [laughs]. We were driven by their desire to have more episodes. Then he called *again* and asked us if the second hour could be expanded to 90 minutes [laughs]! Even though the show is serialized, each episode sort of lands on an ending, in this case [with *Exodus Pts. one & two*], we thought, 'Let's really make it a distinct two-parter.' We saw this as an opportunity to ramp up the finale and make it more theatrical."

BITE CLUB

With all the perils facing the survivors on the island, you would've thought that the open water would be a nice hassle-free break. Not so for Jin, Michael and Sawyer. After a band of strangers abducted Walt and destroyed their raft, Mother Nature sent her most frightening oceanic predator their way. Visual Effects Supervisor KEVIN BLANK, Co-Writer of *Adrift*, LEONARD DICK, and Executive Producer BRYAN BURK get their teeth into *Lost*'s gripping shark attack sequence…

"The shark was a way to raise the emotional context for this relationship. It creates a real danger... it's the two enemies, in effect, having to work together."
— Leonard Dick (Co-Writer)

With the variety of dangers popping up on the *Lost* island, it's easy to forget that those beautiful, blue waters surrounding that crazy rock aren't exactly safe either. Sawyer (Josh Holloway), Jin (Daniel Dae Kim), Michael (Harold Perrineau) and Walt (Malcolm David Kelley) learned that the hard way at the end of season one and the beginning of season two, when their raft journey to civilization was cut short by the appearance of a band of strangers on a tugboat. In the dead of night, on those now ominously black ocean waters, a gun shot rung out, followed by Walt's kidnapping and an explosion that decimated the raft, leaving Jin missing and Michael and Sawyer floating on the wreckage, wounded and emotionally devastated. Angry with one another and both basking in their own guilt, their conflict comes to a head in the episode, *Adrift*, written by Leonard Dick and Steven Maeda. Floating on tiny pieces of the raft, the two men not only have to deal with one another and the elements, but then suddenly there's a fin poking out of the water and next thing you know, the *Jaws* theme is starting to play in everyone's head.

The climactic sequence with Michael and Sawyer facing a hungry shark was a nail-biting highlight of season two's beginnings, with the characters of *Lost* yet again facing nature at its most fierce. Of course, pitching an actual shark against their actors isn't the smartest move, so the *Lost* writers and producers had to come up with some TV magic to make the whole scene come together.

Going back to the story motivations, Co-Writer Leonard Dick reveals that the writers were actually more interested in the emotion of the scene rather than the fish menace. "It was less about the shark and more about Michael and Sawyer. Their relationship had reached a boiling point, where Michael blamed Sawyer [for lighting the flare], while Sawyer cannot believe that Michael is pinning the blame on him, even though deep down he probably does feel guilty for firing that gun and causing Walt to be abducted. The shark was a way to raise the emotional context for this relationship. It creates a real danger and when we get to this climactic sequence, it's the two enemies, in effect, having to work together. Sawyer risks his life and relies on Michael, who absolutely hates him, to protect him. We felt emotionally, that was a very meaty area to explore."

Discussing the sequence's evolution, Dick continues, "We knew that they were going to be on the raft, but there's the old TV rule that two people talking is boring. We knew they were going to return to the island and there had to be obstacles and danger along the way, as with any story. What was interesting for us was that we've had 'monsters', we've had polar bears and French women, but we hadn't explored a *natural* danger. It's funny, we did 25 hours of TV last year and the shark was the first organic danger – it was something you would expect to find in the ocean. We thought it was interesting to create a danger that was native to where they were."

With that, the shark sequence was outlined and it then fell to the location crew in Hawaii and the post-production team to make the writers' vision come to life. "The great thing about our production crew and our visual effects crew is that we never censor ourselves with them. In many ways, they are Dr. Yes," Dick chuckles. "It's also the way we presented it at script stage, which was, 'the danger you don't see is scarier than the danger that you do see.' It's interesting because Steve Maeda, who co-wrote the episode with me, did a shark story on *CSI: Miami*. Their shark was in the daytime, and there were a lot of production issues about how to shoot it and make it realistic. We had the advantage of our two characters being on the raft at night, but again, the focus was less about the shark and more about what was happening between Michael and Sawyer. We spent most of our time and energy on trying to find the best relationship story between these two characters and less on the mechanics of the shark sequence."

"The one thing that the puppeteered fins did that worked well, was create a water displacement and that is very, very complicated to create in CG."
— Kevin Blank (Visual Effects Supervisor)

The mechanics then became the problem of the producers, episode Director, Stephen Williams and Visual Effects Supervisor, Kevin Blank. Bryan Burk, Executive Producer for *Lost*, admits that doing a scene with a shark immediately brought to mind the classic film *Jaws*, which became an intimidating issue for them creatively. "*Jaws* is one of my favorite films and I just knew that when we were doing it, there was no way we could do anything even a tenth as good as *Jaws*," Burk laughs. "Obviously, we wanted to deal with the possibility of the danger in the water and the shark, so the idea was to do it as simplistically and subtly as possible. We're not even close to [Spielberg's] level of greatness, so we tried to stay as far away from *Jaws* as possible. Other than the idea of a shark in the water, I was fearful of any similarities whatsoever because we couldn't come close to it. Even our homage would be embarrassingly inferior to his work, so we stayed as far away as possible!"

Detailing the shoot in Hawaii, Burk reveals, "All of our ocean stuff is shot in the ocean, on the rafts. Our actors often get sea sick, as do our crew and in that respect, if it's possible to have more awe and respect for Spielberg and his crew, I do after watching these scenes."

Burk continues, "Steven Williams, who directed it, did a great job. The question became how to create sharks in places where there were intentionally no sharks? Like, there is a shot looking up at the surface and we put in the shark swimming by, but it was not originally shot for a shark. It was done after the fact. We had decided to have the shark swim by really close, and that was all done with visual effects, but that wasn't the original intention. Steven gave us this great footage and we were able to manipulate it and use it to our advantage. Also, for a lot of it, we started shooting it more practically, and when we got into the editing room, we realized how much more difficult it was to sell the shark, particularly the practical shark. So a lot of the visual effects and the ideas came up in the editing room on how we were going to sell the shark [to the audience] with Kevin Blank after the fact."

For Kevin Blank, it's all in a day's work for his team to be given the task to make a difficult scene work better through the magic of CGI and visual effects, and such was the case with the shark sequence. "They wanted to have a shark sequence and asked, 'Can you do one?' and I said, 'Yes, I can,'" Blank chuckles. "We have a pretty small visual effects budget on the show, so the concern is not always what we can and cannot do, but how much of it we do. Each shot has a certain cost and so we're always trying to be very judicious with the moments when we show something off and then how else we try to sell it, whether it's with other camera angles or drama. We, more or less, were saying we were going to do two CGI shark shots and then we were going to do everything else in camera movement and POVs. Ultimately, it ended up being about six shots! The same thing happened last season with a CGI polar bear sequence, where we set out to do two shots and we ended up with about six or seven!"

Explaining how the sequence ballooned in size, Blank says, "What happened was that we were trying to do some practical elements of a practical shark fin moving through the water, essentially having a puppeteer move it through the water and then not have that as a visual effects shot. It didn't look the way people wanted it to. They didn't like the way it looked and it wasn't moving fast enough, so we decided to cover up the puppeteered fins with CGI fins. The one thing that the puppeteered fins did that worked well, was create a water displacement and that is very, *very* complicated to create in CG."

Blank details the shots that ended up completing the sequence. "We had two fin shots and one underwater shot where you saw [the shark] pass in front of the camera. There was some underwater work done for that, and it was shot during the day and timed darker so we could have enough exposure underwater. It was supposed to be largely POVs and they wanted a shot where a shark moves through the water. Everyone thought the shark looked cool, but we were trying to not necessarily tip that it was a shark, so we pushed it really close to the camera. Everyone sees it and knows it's a shark but we wanted it to be a bit vague, or at least have people say, "Well, I *think* that's what it is." I'll tell you, there was a lot of discussion about what to show and what not to show, because it was a big decision," Blank offers mysteriously.

"We also had another overhead shot where you saw a shape moving under the water, which I believe was an act break. You see Michael and Sawyer on the raft and then the shape moves underneath them. When Michael starts shooting the gun, there is jeopardy that the shark is after Sawyer and Michael kills it, or at least scares it away, with the gun. We wanted the audience to know that it got stopped, so we wanted to see blood, which was a little tricky. The production team had done things like little splashes in the water and what we did was just color that water red. We just dialed in a little red in the computer to simulate blood splattering."

Did the finished sequence and episode capture the look and spirit of what the writers intended? Leonard Dick says, "We were thrilled at the end! Stephen Williams, who directed it, is a pro. It's funny, when you watch these things in dailies, you watch a shot here and a shot there and there's no music. You hear 'action' and see a fin swim by and that kind of thing. It's entirely a credit to our director and our editors on how the final product looks. It's entirely about the directing and the cutting and they did a spectacular job. It just came together beautifully and we were very pleased."

LOVE, HONOR & OBEY

Communication, trust and honesty are considered pretty important factors of any successful marriage. Enter: Jin and Sun – secrets run through their veins as much as their love for one another. DANIEL DAE KIM and YUNJIN KIM unite to talk about *Lost*'s troubled couple...

שׁוּבֵבוּ יַמֵּנוּ יְמַעֲגָּל־צְדָק מְעֵשׂוּ

After

surviving Ocean Airlines Flight 815's turbulent crash, what could be more devastating than being stranded on the island? The obvious answers are becoming a jungle chew-toy for the unstoppable unseen 'monster,' or being assaulted and slaughtered by the ruthless Others. However, pose the same question to actors Daniel Dae Kim and Yunjin Kim (and before you wonder, no, they are not related) and the duo might respond that having their non-English speaking married characters, Jin and Sun Kwon, reduced to stereotypes of some kind is the worse case scenario. "Yunjin and I sat down with Damon Lindelof and J.J. Abrams during the shooting of the pilot and just discussed the pitfalls of the characters," recalls Daniel. "In the first few episodes, these characters were pretty one-dimensional and Jin was especially very unlikable. That was a concern of mine for the Asian American and Korean communities, because I knew they would be watching the show closely. A lot of our discussions centered around the notion of what was going to happen in the future. J.J. and Damon took a lot of time to reassure us that what you see is not what you are going to get. It is important, because we are not represented in a way I feel is demonstrative of our roles here in America and who we really are," says Daniel of the feedback. "So often, we are asked to play characters that are stereotypical, one-dimensional, and not positive representatives of who we are. Until we can get a fully balanced portrayal of our people, I feel it is something I should take into consideration whenever I take a role."

Yunjin echoed similar sentiments and credits the creative team for alleviating those fears. "It is very important and we are lucky to have producers who will not ever let it happen," she offers. "They don't want to add to any stereotype. Not only for us two, but with Sayid too. They are not about to make the guy from Iraq the terrorist bad guy. They would never let that happen. We have producers with open eyes that are way too smart."

As the seemingly meek and timid home-maker Sun, Yunjin is a far cry from home. Referred to as "Korea's Julia Roberts" by *People Magazine* – "That is something I feel uncomfortable about," sighs Yunjin – the beautiful Hollywood newcomer was already a bonafide mega movie star in her native land before ABC snatched Yunjin up. While the casting agents scrambled to fill *Lost*'s ranks, the creators requested she read for Kate since it was the only part available. "Next thing I knew, they were going to write me a role, Sun, and asked me if I would do it," explains Yunjin. "I said, 'Well, yeah! I would love to do it!' As an actor, it is the biggest compliment you can get, especially coming from those guys. I was a huge fan of *Alias* so I knew J.J.'s style from that. It was pretty much a no brainer. I wanted to see if I could make it out here [in the US] and here was this opportunity to make the transition. I said, 'Put me on! Why not?'"

Yet Yunjin reports getting a handle on Sun's quiet and submissive nature was a difficult task. "My nickname, which still exists in Korea, is 'The Girl with the Gun,'" confesses Yunjin "They've called me 'The Woman Warrior.' It is a nickname from a movie I was in called *Shiri* which truly made my career in Korea. So I've never had to play a character that was weak – I don't think Sun's weak, but I don't have a better word for it. In the beginning, I didn't know what to do with Sun. I had to find a way to make her interesting when she doesn't say much, especially when I was only speaking Korean. In scene after scene, Jin barks at her and Sun has her eyes down, hearing, 'Button up the shirt!'"

EVOLUTION

DANIEL DAE KIM discusses nurturing the synergy between *Lost*'s stars…

"It comes from the top down. When we were shooting the pilot, J.J. Abrams and Damon Lindelof created such an inviting, creative atmosphere that it couldn't help but spill over into all of us. I have another theory. As the characters on the show were all stranded on the island, I think all the actors were brought over here to do this particular project for a reason. Maybe that has something to do with why we are gelling so well. My reason is hard to say and I'm still trying to figure it out."

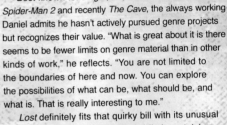

In contrast, *House of the Rising Sun* thrust Jin and Sun into center stage and shattered those preconceptions. Viewers were treated to small glimpses of defiance and as Sun slapped Jin in anger, the flashback episode cemented that she was in charge of her own destiny. "I liked that she wasn't always traditional, but more of a normal girl who, like all women, wanted to find a partner in life and wished for the best," offers Yunjin. "It is odd because she is the one from a wealthy family and decides to give up her life. She cares so much for Jin that in the beginning of their marriage, to make him feel equal, she over-compensated to make him feel like more of a man. On the island, it was like, why is she letting him step all over her? Why does she stay with him?'"

It was a subject Sun has contemplated before. Prior to boarding the fateful flight, she was close to leaving Jin and Yunjin was immediately attracted to that conflict and her alter ego's big secret. "What intrigued me about Sun is her pretending not to speak English," she comments. "I knew from the beginning that she was hiding it from her husband and other people for a reason. But they didn't tell me why. I feel Sun has grown a lot on the island as she started out so submissive."

To facilitate that growth and to compliment Sun, Daniel was brought onboard as her proud husband, Jin. "I did have to audition," says Daniel. "I was different from some of the other cast members in that they didn't create a character around me. They had a specific idea of what they needed for a particular character and I happened to be the person that matched that idea."

Best known for *Angel*, *24*, and feature films *Spider-Man 2* and recently *The Cave*, the always working Daniel admits he hasn't actively pursued genre projects but recognizes their value. "What is great about it is there seems to be fewer limits on genre material than in other kinds of work," he reflects. "You are not limited to the boundaries of here and now. You can explore the possibilities of what can be, what should be, and what is. That is really interesting to me."

Lost definitely fits that quirky bill with its unusual events and complex main figures. Jin is certainly one of the most complex castaways. Although embarrassed by his poor upbringing, he fell head over heels for Sun. She wanted to elope, he convinced her wealthy father to bless their wedding in return for Jin joining the family business. Not realizing what that entailed, Jin became sucked into Mr. Paik's seedy and violent affairs and consequently, grew more distant from his soul mate.

"Everything surprised me," confirms Daniel about his history. "When we started the series, we didn't know much about our characters' back-stories. I ended up creating my character's own back-story, biography, history, and childhood. I was really surprised to see so much of it was different from what I envisioned. That is a testament to how talented the writers are."

Jin disapproved of Mr. Paik's shady affairs, so what did sticking it out prove? "It says how much he loves his wife," says Daniel. "At the core of everything he's done, it is out of love and the intensity of feeling he has for her. He sacrificed his own ambition and family for her. Making a sacrifice out of love is noble in the end."

ABANDONED

Could Sun have left Jin for another man? DANIEL DAE KIM certainly believes so…

"I thought the writers were going to go down a road of Michael and Sun having a romantic relationship. When we were reading the scripts, I was seeing these kinds of clues but it flipped around. What the writers have said publicly is it partially has to do with Harold and I being good friends off set. They saw chemistry between the two of us and altered the storyline. That is part of the talent of our writers and producers. They not only have strong ideas about what characters can do, but they are also open and willing to see what the individual actors bring to the table."

"My nickname, which still exists in Korea, is 'The Woman Warrior.' It is a nickname from a movie I was in called Shiri which truly made my career in Korea."
— Yunjin Kim

However, snapping, "I will tell you what to do!" to Sun, Jin has come off as possessive, over bearing, and a bit of an ass at times. "I've been told that many times," muses Daniel. "It was problematic for me to play someone like that, and if that was all he was going to be, I wouldn't have taken the role."

Yet during the early days, Jin wasn't necessarily a team player. Being an outsider who refused to socialize with anyone other than his wife, Jin instigated his fair share of misunderstandings. Most notorious was his intense brawl with Michael over a watch. The one-sided beating resulted in Jin being handcuffed to the plane wreckage and to rectify the situation, Sun confided in Michael. "Michael was the only character who knew Sun spoke English but she asked him not to tell anybody else, especially Jin," explains Yunjin. "He kept his promise and it's not until episode 17 that she revealed that she can speak English. Waiting around for that was a bit frustrating because even though I love working with Daniel, it would have been nice to mix and match sometimes. And it was like 'When is this going to happen?' but it was just a matter of time. *Lost* is a huge puzzle."

The two men clashed once again when Michael's raft went up in smoke and Jin is accused of sabotaging their ticket off the island. "I loved it!" exclaims Yunjin. "Tucker Gates [below] was directing that episode and did a wonderful job of actually doing a slow motion of the whole fight scene, then getting back to Sun's face to see how long she is going to wait to burst out in English, 'Stop! Leave him alone!' It was just building until she screamed those lines out. I thought it was brilliant."

> *"Sun cares so much for Jin that in the beginning of their marriage, to make him feel equal, she over-compensated. On the island, it was like, why is she letting him step all over her?"*
> — Yunjin Kim

Unfortunately, Jin wasn't so grateful and feeling betrayed, declared it too late to mend their marriage. "There is absolutely a lot of resentment," agrees Daniel. "Love and hate are so closely related because they are both emotions of passion. The more you love someone, the more you can hate the same person. The fact that he sacrificed all these things, found out she spoke English, and was going to leave him... so sure, they have issues to work out."

Ironically, Michael and Jin gradually formed a friendship after that dispute. "It is more than just tolerating each other," explains Daniel. "They probably see similarities in their circumstances. In the end, Jin offers to help Michael build his boat because he is sorry for what he's done and how he's treated him. This is one of the strange things about this island: the strongest of enemies become the best of friends. There is willingness on both of their parts to turn over a new page and start again."

Taking a cue from his spouse, Jin runs away (well, sails away) with Sawyer, Michael, and Walt instead of tackling his marital woes. "That is part of the motivation of him being on the raft," states Daniel. "There are others as well. Trying to find help, in a way, he feels he is contributing. This is probably foremost in his mind. Because of his lack of communication skills, he feels the need to contribute in some other way. Building this raft and getting out to sea is something that is active and physical and doesn't require sophisticated communication."

Sun and Jin have gone through 'relationship hell and back' and the pinnacle was the teary eyed farewell on the beach, a scene Daniel is particularly pleased with. "Although I've worked on a lot of shows, films, and done a lot of stage, there are very few times in my career where I've been asked to have such an intense emotional scene. That is one of the reasons I am so grateful to be on a show like this. Asian American men are very rarely seen as people with romantic lives and people who feel deeply. That scene with Sun was notable because I got to do scenes I'd seen other actors do, but hadn't got the chance to do myself. Also, it was great for the character because we hadn't seen Jin be tender to his wife, apologizing, and expressing love. It was pretty memorable to me."

In *Lost*'s year one cliffhanger, the raft finally shoved off with disastrous results. Relatively vulnerable on the open water, strangers soon attacked – Sawyer was shot, Walt kidnapped, and Jin disappeared under the waves. Filming such watery sequences can be exhausting, but after training for the underwater creature feature *The Cave*, Daniel dived right in. "I actually enjoyed them a little more than I though I would," he grins. "Generally, I don't get sea-sick and for some reason, the water in Hawaii is a lot less intimidating to me than waters in the Atlantic Ocean that are green and murky. We were out there and could see the bottom so I felt really safe out there. That is not to say there weren't challenges, because we were out there for a good long time in the middle of the night without a lot of sleep. I was glad to have done it that way because if we were to have shot that stuff in a studio, it would have been completely apparent and non realistic."

Their little adventure, including being captured by the Tailies and thrown into a pit, cultivated a special bond and established Jin as a fiercely loyal character, a quality Daniel and the writers had discussed. "We see him carry Sawyer with Michael, saying he won't leave Sawyer, and going after Michael," says Daniel. "It is a great characteristic in Jin that he does a lot for the people he cares for. It takes a little while for people to break through his armor but once they do, he goes a long way in making sure he treats them with respect and honor. It is an interesting reminder of how far Jin has come in his ability to relate to others. When he first got to the island, you saw how cold and standoffish he was to everybody. This time, he wasn't as fearful and was a lot more active with them. It was a positive step for him."

HUMBLE HAWAII

YUNJIN KIM on the benefits of filming on the island...

"People here don't make a big deal about us. Sometimes I need to go to Los Angeles or New York to feel like, 'Oh yeah... I guess we're a hit!' Shooting out here, we don't feel it. I don't even need sunglasses like when I go to Korea or a major city. Sometimes you enjoy people coming up and saying how much they love the show, and other times you want privacy, especially when you just got up and haven't had your coffee. Here, I don't care. I just walk out and there is something mellow about this place. We can concentrate on our work here."

LOST LIKE TEARS IN RAIN

After tapping into her tear reservoirs for Sun, YUNJIN KIM would like to dry her eyes…

"Sun is a very emotional character and sometimes I ask if we can cut back on the emotional stuff. So every time we have a script where I am going through some emotional trauma, I ask, 'Can we cut it down because last episode I was crying too.' With the director, I usually set out and make sure we don't play the emotional part over and over, and to save it until we really need it."

Back on the beach, it was impossible to keep optimistic when all signs pointed otherwise. "When Claire shows Sun the bottle, Sun pretty much thinks: the raft is gone, and her husband is gone and dead out at sea," says Yunjin. "It's been very traumatic." Naturally, Sun was overwhelmed when her missing husband walked back into her life. "To see him come out while Sun was doing laundry…" says Yunjin. "In the script, it said 'very emotional reunion type of embrace.' I said to the director, 'She would be too shocked with the turmoil inside her.' It is such a surprise that he is walking towards her like a dream. She can't believe it, so that is how we decided to shoot this. We made a good decision."

The two reconciled but don't count on a fairy tale ending. "I am sure the writers will come up with a brilliant thing to fight about or to fall out over for a couple of episodes," comments Yunjin. "Drama is conflict. If they are happy, it is not very interesting. But none of us know. That is why when we get the scripts, we rip through them wherever we are."

"At the core of all Jin's done, it is out of love and the intensity of feeling he has for Sun. He sacrificed his own ambition and family for her. Making a sacrifice out of love is noble in the end."
— Daniel Dae Kim

"This is one of the strange things about this island: the strongest of enemies become the best of friends. There is a willingness to turn over a new page and start again."
– Daniel Dae Kim

Expectations are flying high so what's coming up next on *Lost*? If they know, neither actor is spilling the dirt. It's all so hush-hush that they aren't even in the loop themselves. However, Yunjin is in favor of such secrecy, maintaining it keeps them on their toes and safe from Freudian slips. "None of us know," confirms Yunjin. "We don't know when the next victim is going to die. I would rather not know anyway. If I knew, even though I'd be acting, the camera never lies. Even though I'd try my best to keep on a poker face, I might hint or there might be something subconscious going on in my mind. With the type of audience we have on *Lost*, they are so smart and keen. They even pick up things I miss. When the shark went by with the Dharma insignia, I didn't even know until a couple of days later. I was on set and they were talking about it. I was 'What do you mean?' They were like 'You didn't see it?' I was like, 'No, and I watched the episode. What are you talking about?' It was something that happened last minute and wasn't in the script. It happened during editing stages and was an idea the producers came up with."

Nothing seems set in stone so if the powers-that-be are listening, both actors have a few suggestions. To date, Sun has sat on the sidelines when it comes to unraveling the island's mysteries, so Yunjin is aching for some excitement or, heck, to even be put in mortal danger. "I would love to!" she says. "Sun needs to climb a tree. I am the only character who has always been safe. I am never running away from anything so I keep on saying to the producers, 'I think I am the only one who didn't hear those odd whispers on the island.' I can run and I can't wait for that to happen, whether it is from the 'monster', the Others, or a polar bear."

As for Jin's future, Daniel notes, "I'm looking forward to seeing him continue in the direction he's going. Seeing him more integral to the group and the fabric of this society is a really positive step. All of us need to find our role in the group and contribute. I am also looking forward to him speaking more English because that is a key to that integration."

Indeed. So far, Jin has only mastered a few key English phrases and Daniel confirms performing in Korean has been one of the biggest challenges in his extensive career. "Although it is my first language, it is not the one I am most comfortable with," says Daniel. "It just means my preparation has to start earlier than it normally does. I have to think more about the intention and pronunciation of the lines which I'm not used to. It is also a great opportunity because my Korean has improved tremendously. I am really proud to be able to speak the language of my ancestors."

It also forces him to connect more with sight than sound. "I have to rely a lot more on my non-verbal communication skills," agrees Daniel. "That way, it feels like stage work, because I am communicating with my whole body. Usually when I'm on the screen, I let my words and eyes do the work but here, I have to do more than that."

In the past, Daniel was slaughtered on *Angel*, impaled in *The Cave*, and was voted most likely to meet a grisly end first on the island. Daniel dodged that bullet and is now hoping to keep death at bay and possibly stay *Lost* forever. "I've heard Damon and J.J. say in a number of interviews that the audience needs to be reminded of the stakes," he concludes. "This is a life or death situation. The reality is being on the island, your chance of survival isn't the same as living in a quiet suburb on the main land. That said, I love being on the show and hopefully Jin has honed up on his survival skills enough to last for a while."

UNITY

Since the two share the majority of their onscreen time together, YUNJIN KIM and DANIEL DAE KIM have naturally left everlasting impressions on each other…

"Yunjin is a really talented actress and a true professional," praises Daniel. "She makes it very easy to work with her. Not only is she prepared and in the moment, but she's also very gracious when working together. When you are playing with someone like that, all you need to do is react, play along, and something wonderful will come out of that."

Needless to say, Yunjin has similar admiration for Daniel. When he popped up on *People Magazine*'s 'Sexiest Men of 2005' list, she wasn't the least bit surprised. "I went and voted for him online," notes Yunjin. "He was number nine, and I was like 'Nooooo!' I emailed everyone. I didn't expect number one, but come on!" she smiles. "We are hardly ever serious. We are so comfortable, we joke around, and I love that chemistry. I became friends with him, his wife, and their kids."

FLIGHT PLAN

Courtesy of the *Lost* Production Office we present to you the original concept art for Oceanic Flight 815's wreckage, designed March 2004, prior to shooting *Lost*'s pilot episode...

"LOST" - BEACH CRASH SITE — REAR OF FUSELAGE.

CLOCKWISE FROM FAR
LEFT: Front view of the
main crash site; side view
of the wreckage showing
the island coastline; rear
section of the fuselage;
and the original concept of
how the crashed cockpit
might look in the jungle

"LOST" FRONT FUSELAGE preliminary 02/23/04

The
Oceanic

תעד לפני, שלתר נגד צררי חישגת בשמו ראשי, כוסי

73

EKO LOCATION

Just as Locke thinks he's the only survivor who trusts destiny, along comes a goliath who embraces spirituality and fate, in the quietly imposing form of Mr. Eko. ADEWALE AKINNUOYE-AGBAJE takes five by the fire and reveals the journey that led him to the island…

Any fan of *Lost* knows that there's a yin for every yang on the island inhabited by the survivors of Oceanic Flight 815. As Boone died, Claire gave birth to Aaron. Michael and Walt were torn apart, while Jin and Sun were reunited. Even Jack's predisposition to trust in science is balanced by Locke's unshakable faith. So it's really no surprise then that one of the newest character additions to the series is a man that truly embodies the fascinating dichotomy of the island – the mysterious Mr. Eko. Large and imposing in stature, yet gentle of soul, Mr. Eko has revealed himself over the season to be a study in contrasts. A past involvement with drug deals and men of the cloth, like the best characters on *Lost*, he is proving to be a complex composition that defies stereotypes. Played with intensity and quiet grace by British actor Adewale Akinnuoye-Agbaje, the character of Mr. Eko not only managed to captivate audiences, but also the imagination of the mercurial actor who was initially reticent about taking on the role and joining the castaways of *Lost*.

"At the time *Lost* came to me, I wasn't interested too much in acting and I certainly wasn't interested in TV, because I like my freedom and I don't like to be locked down," Akinnuoye-Agbaje details from his home in Hawaii. A man of many talents, including lawyer, model, actor and writer, Adewale spent the last decade crafting roles in films like *Congo*, and the television series *Oz*, before *Lost* came knocking. "I had actually taken three years off from the profession," he continues. "I got a little burned out and I wanted to get in touch with some of the other things I wanted to do, like writing or getting behind the camera. I sat out for a while and at the beginning of [2005], I came out with a couple of films, just because financially I needed to get the ball rolling again and I'd been out of the game. I did a few films, *Mistress of the Spices* and *Get Rich or Die Tryin'*. I did them simply because I was writing a project I intended to direct and produce and act in and I used all my resources in getting that project to the forefront, so I needed financially to get back in the game. I also felt at this point it was a good idea to get a little bit of visibility that would facilitate me getting my project on the map. So I was definitely not interested in committing to a TV series, because that long-term thing would push my own project off too far."

Luckily for Akinnuoye-Agbaje, his diligent manager pushed the actor to take a look at what *Lost* was offering him. "I hadn't even heard of the series because in London it hadn't aired at the time. This came across the table and he called me very excited and he said it was pitch perfect TV. Again, I was very reluctant. But at the end of shooting *Get Rich or Die Tryin'*, Carlton [Cuse, Executive Producer on *Lost*] expressed an interest in meeting me. I met him in New York and he pitched the project and told me what the concept was. He gave me the DVDs to watch and I liked the way they shot the series and it was quite interesting, but I had played an African character for four years and I had just broken the mold from that by playing an American lead in *Get Rich or Die Tryin'* and I was very happy to have gotten out of that realm and now this was going to pull me back in. I told Carlton I didn't really want to play another Nigerian. He just said, 'Damon, would like to have a chat with you' and they flew me out to L.A. I had a sit down with Damon and he explained to me some of his ideas in more depth, like the priest issues and how they wanted to represent more of a benevolent and pure spiritual force of the island through this character. It presented a challenge that I was quite intrigued with in my own life. I'm a Buddhist and I thought it would be a great opportunity to explore a spiritual realm even deeper, of my faith and other people's. I've always been intrigued with mystical spiritual characters and I've never played a priest and I thought it would be great to go there and study the Bible in the environment of Hawaii, which has a very mystic energy. It's very powerful and I thought it was a great opportunity that I shouldn't turn down. I didn't have to audition and they offered me the part. It was a wonderful tribute and I thought about it and even though I was exhausted from the last film, I said, 'Yeah, let's give it a shot.' I had no idea what I was saying

LOST CONNECTION

Akinnuoye-Agbaje arrived in Hawaii last summer and hit the island running. "Initially, it was overwhelming!" the actor admits with a sigh. "The shift from London, which was where I was based, was a huge relocation. I was used to doing movies where they house you and get you a car, etc. They baby you through the process so you can get on with the work. With this, relocation was achieved and I understood what the word meant," he laughs. "I had to find a house and buy a new car. The producer Jean Higgins said to me, 'Look, here's a map – go out there and get lost. It's the best advice I can give you, because once you get lost, you find your way.' I remember the second day, I was given a map to this place an hour away and I had to be up at four in the morning to drive there and I had never been on the island. I had no real time to think. It was a case of jumping right in and getting on with the work. I needed at first to get a real grip and crux with the character and that was my focus, so I jumped into a hotel and put aside looking for an apartment. And once I got in and understood the thru-line of the character, I started to feel a bit comfortable."

"Harold [Perrineau] told me the best places to live and the best place to pick up a car. In fact, I'm not living too far from him now, so we are virtually neighbors. It was nice that I knew somebody and we are from the same walk of life. I wasn't a total stranger. The funny thing is that when I was shooting *Get Rich* in New York, Harold was on hiatus and we actually met and we both went to see another actor friend of ours from *Oz*. I remember Harold saying he was doing this show called *Lost* and how he missed us guys because he was way out there and he'd love for us to be out there with him. I had no idea a couple months later, I'd be living right next door to him! I have to watch what that guy says now, he has a certain power to his words."

— Adewale Akinnuoye-Agbaje

Mr. Eko was dramatically introduced in the final moments of season two's *Adrift* and in subsequent episodes was revealed to be with the rest of the tail survivors of the Oceanic crash. Akinnuoye-Agbaje remembers starting the work on his character in those initial days on the set was especially intense. "We came up with the original concept of [the character] who was named Emeka. I changed it to Mr. Eko, and Damon was great and loved the idea. We came up with the initial concept, but as soon as I got here and they saw how I performed among the other actors, it completely changed," he smiles. "It can be a frustrating process if you are a person that likes to be somewhat in control and know what you are doing, which is what I have been. The only way it becomes rewarding is to literally let go and be in the moment, because they are giving you scripts every week where you don't know what you are going to be doing. The only way to flourish is to embrace it."

"*The shift from London was a huge relocation. I had to find a house and buy a new car. Producer Jean Higgins said to me, 'Look, here's a map – go out there and get lost. It's the best advice I can give you, because once you get lost, you find your way.*"

"The whole back-story has got everything – sexiness, power, intense aggression, passion, compassion, beauty and there's crying and killing and laughing!"

BARRISTER ORIGINS?

Fortunately, he had his fellow Tailies to share in the process of acclimating and getting comfortable with the rigors of the show. "I remember the first day of work for me was my birthday and they bought me a cake and I shared it with every member of the cast and crew and that was a great way of being introduced to the family. But there was so much to do and very little time to actually socialize and integrate with the entire cast outside from the work. It kind of helped me zone in the first couple of months, as I just shot with the Tailies. It was a wonderful, organic process of natural bonding with Michelle Rodriguez, Cynthia [Watros] and the other actors. I didn't do a scene with the other island members for a good two months, so we really did have that feeling that we were on a different side of the island and were a different group. We developed our own nuances, so when we did finally get to perform with some of the established cast, it was kind of a weird relationship, because it was very much, 'Who are these people?'" he laughs. "It felt like a different series and it was naturally a good position to be in because it was genuine."

In particular, Adewale says he and his comrade in the jungle, actress Michelle Rodriguez [Ana Lucia], have connected strongly, just like their characters on the series. "She is a wonderful person and a wonderful actor. I really and truly enjoy working with her. The relationship that we have with the characters is kind of what we have with ourselves. It's one of mutual respect and we have our certain ways of doing things, but we still respect each other as to how we go about it. Michelle and I decided on pursuing our natural bond, the organic bond we would have in that jungle and how we would feel with each other and put it into the characters."

Now months into his time at *Lost*, Adewale readily admits the greatest challenge hasn't been the bugs, long hours or physical stunts – it's all about trust. "I've never been really great at trusting anybody just because of the way I grew up. I was always led to believe you should take care of yourself, trust in your own abilities and you're the author of your own destiny. Coming to this show is the opposite," he laughs. "I have to really trust that these writers and creators are going to really flesh this character out and address all of the issues that are dear to me and to them and not make him a one-dimensional caricature. It was a process in the early stages but especially with the back-story now, they've got me in their hands and I fully trust them."

Eko's past was finally revealed in the episode, *The 23rd Psalm* and Akinnuoye-Agbaje is genuine in his praise of the story. "It is a fabulous script, just genius, but it's completely off of what we discussed," he laughs. "When I got it, I was like, 'Wait a minute! I've been acting all of this and now I'm this?' There was a part of me that said, 'No, I wanted to do *this*,' but then I realized what they've done is take the natural instinctive way that I am, as an individual and an actor, and they've twisted it into their conception. It's not the straight and narrow priest they said. He has a very pure, benevolent nature, cut and dry, black and white kind of guy. I thought it was great, that I can be a priest and my perception was a 'by all means necessary' priest. Then all of a sudden, he's a bleedin' drug dealer! I was like, 'No, I played one of those for four years!' The reason I took the part was to avoid that, but then I saw the way that it was woven and it was ingenious. They made this guy somebody that was a tortured priest and he may have always been a priest in his life, but there was a struggle of when and where he was going to fully embrace it. I was just really impressed with how they'd woven together all the ideas I suggested and my physicality. Damon is a shrewd writer. He really studies the individual and pulls from them and whacks it right into the character. You have to be careful what you say to that guy, because you might see it coming out on the pages," he chuckles. "He's like a vacuum cleaner! He studies you and I mean it in the best possible way, because you are getting to challenge things in your life through the character."

"I was going through colleges as a teenager and it was more of a parental application as opposed to a personal one to pursue law. I studied it and found it very interesting. I specialized in Crime and Criminology. From O's to A levels and then the degree and the Masters, it all took seven years. After that I was like, 'I'm kind of done here.' I was going to go into a PhD and my head was exhausted. I was still quite young and I felt I really wanted to pursue things that were closer to my heart, which was a creative field. I used to paint and draw and that was always in my heart. I wanted to get out into the world and try to explore some of the things I really desired and was interested in. That inspiration led me to acting in a very long, abbreviated way, really. It's a process and I hadn't thought about being an actor. I just knew what I didn't want to do and I kind of followed my nose and it led me here. I wanted to be famous in some degree – to be out there!"
– Adewale Akinnuoye-Agbaje

Adewale says there is another major moment in his mind that defines Eko on the show. "There was this turning point with me and Michelle leading the pack to some degree and then Jin wanted to go run after Michael and it was the first time I said to Ana Lucia I wasn't going to follow her anymore. I wasn't going to play the game of brutal survival by any means necessary. I was going to address my humane and compassionate issues that were dear to me and I was going to help this guy, even if it risks my life and the group. I head-butted Jin to the floor and it was a great moment. It typifies who the character is – he has this beautiful compassion and humanity within him, but he'll knock you out in order to get it across. He'll knock you out for the sweetest of reasons and I thought that was a great curve and turning point. Plus, the whole back-story is the best time I've had shooting on TV and on film. It's got everything I wanted – sexiness, power, intense aggression, passion, compassion, beauty, and there's crying and killing and laughing. It's got everything!" With a happy sigh, he adds, "How the turning point has been manifesting into my back-story is the best gift I've ever had in my career – it's a lovely, lovely web that's been woven and I'm happy to be playing it."

"Two sides. One is light. One is dark"

MAN OF FAITH

At times, the island's most pensive and unassuming resident. At others, a man whose inner fire burns anyone who dares to get too close. TERRY O'QUINN tends to the embers and takes a closer look at the enigma that is John Locke…

"Faith versus science... when people say it that way, it suggests that faith is something that you can't see and have no proof of, when in fact there was plenty of proof that there was something strange and powerful on the island."

LONDON CALLING

TERRY O'QUINN reveals he could be about to re-tread the boards…

"I think I might try to do a summer play in the northeast, or there is talk about me doing a short stint in London. I haven't done a play in 15 years! I can't believe it's been that long. It's all I did when I started my career. It's a great way to charge the batteries."

There's always been a duality

to the nature of John Locke. In those first hours on the beach, amongst the wreckage of Oceanic Flight 815, Locke proved himself to be both a leader, helping to save lives, and a loner, with his odd humor and cryptic conversations.

In the days since, he's evolved and shifted to be many things to many survivors, from a trusted provider and man of admirable faith, to the inadvertent killer of Boone and the increasingly conflicted keeper of the hatch. He's a man that sometimes seems as mercurial as the wind, casting his steady green-eyed gaze upon his fellow brethren with either the eyes of warmest compassion and wisdom, or the cold glare of anger and frustration. Enigmatic to the core, he's also a man reborn by the fateful crash, as revealed when he discovered his miraculous ability to walk, despite being confined to a wheelchair prior to the crash. Now a disciple of the island and the 'gifts' it chooses to reveal to them all, Locke is the voice of faith and the ever-challenging counterpoint to Jack's equally unfailing argument for the 'absolutes of science.'

Even though there have been five Locke-centric flashback episodes so far, the audience is still waiting on pins and needles for his mysteries to be explained. Just don't look for actor Terry O'Quinn to reveal or conjecture what those answers may be. He admits he's blissfully unaware of where John Locke is heading and that works just fine for the charming, down-to-earth actor. It's a fact that hasn't changed since J.J. Abrams called O'Quinn two years ago and asked him to take role on faith alone. That career leap of faith has since rewarded the actor with an Emmy nomination and mainstream recognition from fans around the world. Yet, the self-deprecating actor downplays that initial risk and smiles offering, "Yeah, it was a leap of faith, but just as much as that, the reality of the situation is that I needed a job. It works both ways. It's easier to leap when you are starving and there is something to eat on the other side."

Having spent the last 25 years earning a stellar reputation as a theater, film and television character actor, O'Quinn admits that joining *Lost* was an interesting exercise in trust from the beginning. It was only when he was handed the script to *Walkabout* that he started to get a sense of the potential of the character he had committed himself to. "I was excited by the script, because I thought it was pretty cool and an interesting story," he reflects. "But it didn't really tell me much more about how the show was going to go. It was all still a mystery."

And it has remained a mystery for the actors, since Executive Producers Damon Lindelof and Carlton Cuse have a tendency to not share with them details of what's coming next for their characters. As an ensemble, they've learned to live for the next script. For Terry, it's been a freeing release to play a character in the moment. "All I really brought to the role was my voice, my body, my mind and my heart," he shares. "The rest of it is being shaped by the powers that be. What's good for these characters are the people writing the show. They determine what we play or where we go from here. So I look at each script as a little movie. Some movies I have a lot to do, some movies I don't have a lot to do. All I can relate to is what has happened in the past and I don't even have to do a lot of work in that respect, because the writers do so much of that work for me. I can pretty much act in the immediate time of the script."

While many actors find it difficult to not have detailed motivations for their characters, O'Quinn says he actually prefers the spontaneity. "I don't think it's hard. I think it's easier, because it's less baggage you have to carry. If you know the whole story, well then you've probably planned your whole performance because then you figure two episodes down the line, 'I'm going to get to letter L, so right now I'm going to do letter D this way.' It's your responsibility to try to shape a performance if you have a script that you know the beginning, the middle and the end. But if you don't know the end, you aren't burdened with the responsibility to shape everything towards the end. In that respect, it's easier. It's just like real life, and that's what I kind of love about it. You can go with what you know up to now… you can't go by tomorrow. If you try to plan your performance, you may get choked off just down the road. When people ask what I want to have happen to my character, I say I want my character to have interesting scenes to play. I want to have good scenes and time to play them and that's all I want. If I start having desires and it starts not to go the way I wish it to go, that's creating a disappointment for yourself."

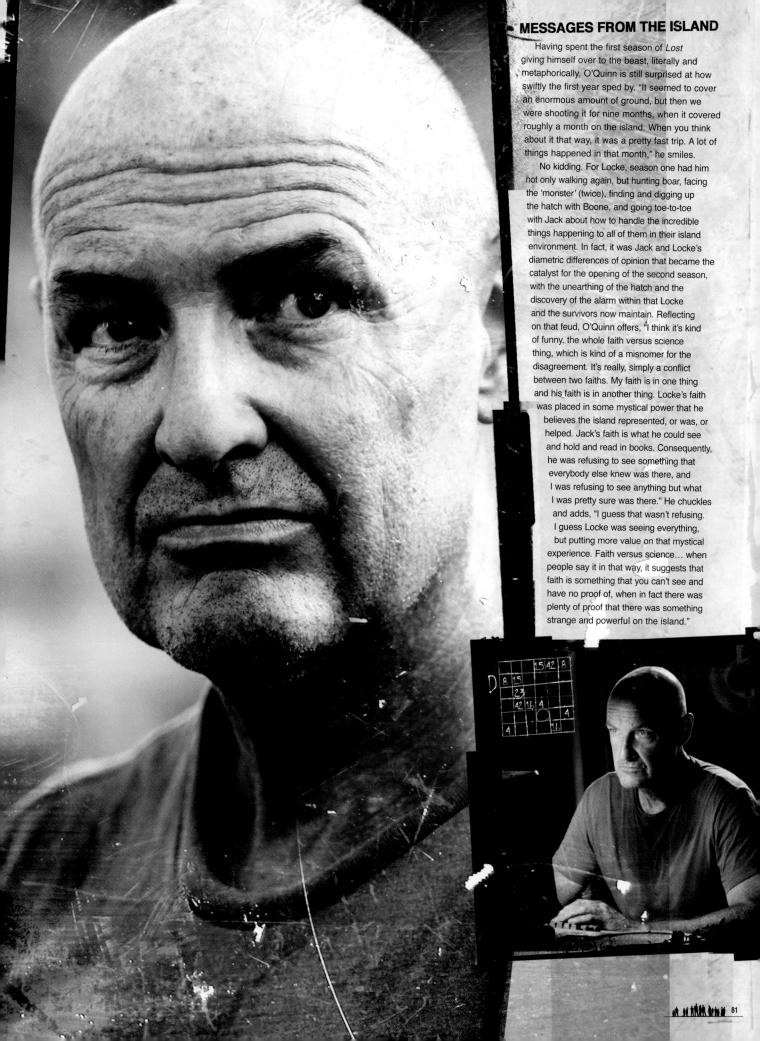

MESSAGES FROM THE ISLAND

Having spent the first season of *Lost* giving himself over to the beast, literally and metaphorically, O'Quinn is still surprised at how swiftly the first year sped by. "It seemed to cover an enormous amount of ground, but then we were shooting it for nine months, when it covered roughly a month on the island. When you think about it that way, it was a pretty fast trip. A lot of things happened in that month," he smiles.

No kidding. For Locke, season one had him not only walking again, but hunting boar, facing the 'monster' (twice), finding and digging up the hatch with Boone, and going toe-to-toe with Jack about how to handle the incredible things happening to all of them in their island environment. In fact, it was Jack and Locke's diametric differences of opinion that became the catalyst for the opening of the second season, with the unearthing of the hatch and the discovery of the alarm within that Locke and the survivors now maintain. Reflecting on that feud, O'Quinn offers, "I think it's kind of funny, the whole faith versus science thing, which is kind of a misnomer for the disagreement. It's really, simply a conflict between two faiths. My faith is in one thing and his faith is in another thing. Locke's faith was placed in some mystical power that he believes the island represented, or was, or helped. Jack's faith is what he could see and hold and read in books. Consequently, he was refusing to see something that everybody else knew was there, and I was refusing to see anything but what I was pretty sure was there." He chuckles and adds, "I guess that wasn't refusing. I guess Locke was seeing everything, but putting more value on that mystical experience. Faith versus science… when people say it in that way, it suggests that faith is something that you can't see and have no proof of, when in fact there was plenty of proof that there was something strange and powerful on the island."

LOST

Strange for certain, with any given script throwing curve ball after curve ball at the actors, what with polar bears, the Others, and black smoke 'monsters', to name only a few. Asked if it's ever too much for him to swallow, O'Quinn offers, "Occasionally. But I am always pretty delighted. The only times I go, 'Wow, you don't see that coming!' is when you see something *else* coming. When you anticipate, the odds are you are going to anticipate wrong. So I never saw me getting dragged through the woods, or the dynamite or the hatch. I didn't think that when Boone and I found a little piece of metal in the ground, and then realized it was a hatch, that would consume us for the second half of the season and, in fact, for most of this season."

Speaking of which, season two has primarily seen Locke entangled in the issues of the hatch and deconstructing the mysteries of the Dharma project, all the while pressing the button every 108 minutes according to schedule. O'Quinn admits going into the hatch has been at once compelling and frustrating for him. "I think Locke is still not sure whether it was a good thing or a bad thing. Now, he's pushing this button and he has to ask himself, 'Is this it then?' One of the wonderful things about this show is that this is a human question. Everyone on Earth always asks: 'Is this it? Why are we here?' 'Why do I act the way that I do?' and 'Does anybody love me?' I think one of the reasons the show is so successful is because it has this small group of people examining those three questions very assiduously."

THE FUSELAGE

The interaction on J.J.'s official *Lost* site, according to TERRY O'QUINN…

"I did The Fuselage all last year and the first half of this year. Then when I and my character began to get frustrated, I didn't feel like I was at the top of my form, so I backed off that and I don't think people know why I backed off. There were too many opinions and I felt like I was getting away from the person I was when I started the show, so I had to step out of that stuff for a while. I feel like I abandoned them to a certain extent. Everybody was very good and supportive there, but there were just too many voices in my head."

Yet on the other hand, the story arc has kept Locke away from the action until only recently. A turn of events that was concerning for the actor. "Personally, I felt like Locke went down the hatch, found the button and he stayed down there for a while and they went and did other things. It's kind of how I felt. I said to the guys, 'Hey, I hope this isn't the answer. I got the button and now that's it for Locke.' I talked to Damon [Lindelof], Carlton [Cuse] and Bryan [Burk] and they said, 'We hear you and we hear Locke.' So, we'll see what happens," he smiles.

This season in flashbacks, Locke's painful history with his father, and his romance with a fellow support group member, Helen, have further defined the tragic elements of the character. With each piece of the puzzle revealed, O'Quinn says he is also sucked into the drama just like the fans. "One of the genius things about this show, whether intentional or not intentional, is that we are exploring his history and his history is taking him to his present. Locke is still looking for something. I have always thought of him as a seeker. He is searching for something – a sense of self. Who am I? And why am I who I am? In fact, he's going to find out when the audience finds out. You kind of go, 'Is he bad or a tragic figure?' but you don't really know until you know the whole story. Until he looks at it and examines it himself, we have to hold our judgment in abeyance." As an example, O'Quinn cites the moment in *Fire + Water*, where Locke violently punches Charlie repeatedly for taking Claire's baby again. "A lot of characters do things and fans go, 'I can't believe that person did that! Why did he do that?' I heard that people said that about [*Fire + Water*], that it was out of character for Locke. Well, it's because we don't know his whole character. From what deep well did that violence, anger and frustration come? The thing about these characters is they only know as much as we know in the audience. It's kind of amazing and kind of unique, I think. It's one of the things that makes it so special."

Aside from the challenges of his storyline, O'Quinn admits the shake-up of the structure in the first third of the second season and the addition of new cast posed a very different set of issues too. "[The show] feels a little bit like a different animal. In all honesty, you get a sense of group and a feel and a shape to an ensemble, and then somebody throws something else in it and there are ripples," he offers. "It changes the shape of the ensemble and it brings in a different feel and different smell… I always think of things in terms of a herd of horses or a pack of wolves!" he chuckles. "So you bring in something else and the vibe changes and it takes a while before that finally gets absorbed and it all gets calm again. It has become a different thing, but it finally gets back to a consistent and regular feeling. It doesn't get back to the same feeling, but at least it gets to what I know now and what I now understand."

"*Locke is still looking for something. I have always thought of him as a seeker. He is searching for something – a sense of self. In fact, he's going to find out when the audience finds out.*"

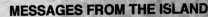

"Everyone on Earth always asks: 'Is this it? Why are we here?' 'Why do I act the way that I do?' and 'Does anybody love me?' I think one of the reasons the show is so successful is because it has this small group of people examining those three questions very assiduously."

PUNCHLINES

TERRY O'QUINN explains his cheeky SAG Award acceptance speech…

"Well, I wanted to say something about that. I get so bored at those things, I thought I might as well do something at least mildly entertaining. You have to have a lot of faith and trust and love in each other to do crap like that and get away with it. It was funny."
And here is O'Quinn's speech that had everybody rolling in the aisles:
"A friend of mine always says, if you don't have something nice to say about someone, let's hear it [laughter]. So, about our cast, I'd like to say that this is the saddest collection of climbing, grasping, paranoid, backstabbing, scene-grabbing losers and schmoozers, [laughter] that you ever saw on stage in your life [applause]. But we love each other very much. And we want to thank our fellow members of the Guild for recognizing us as an ensemble. And we would like to take this singular opportunity to express our gratitude, to J.J. Abrams, and Damon Lindelof, for creating what is clearly an ensemble piece [applause]."

What he does understand is the joy of working with his fellow cast members and seeing them grow in their craft. "I like working with Matthew [Fox] and Dom [Monaghan]," O'Quinn enthuses. "I did theater for a long time and I worked with a lot of old pros and a lot of people who ultimately spoke the same language. In a way, they are almost of my generation, but they're not, yet they have a way of working that I am very familiar with. They are old pros. And Jorge [Garcia] is always throwing curve balls and change-ups and you don't really know if he's really working or not working," he jokes, adding, "He's probably the sweetest man on Earth. Then there is Josh [Holloway], who is just good-natured and very funny, but very serious. He is really concerned with getting things right. He's the same age as Matthew, yet to me he sometimes seems like a really young guy, which is really refreshing. Evangeline [Lilly], I've seen her go from not having any experience, but intuitive skills, and she's grown enormously," he says warmly. "When we started the show with 14 main characters, I didn't imagine we'd be talking to each other by the end of the year. I figured there would be cliques, or this or that, but it's been a treat. I don't think you would get it with 14 other people. I think J.J. either has a wonderful intuition or good luck when he is casting. Partly, that is affected when you bring in new people. It changes it and you think the thing we had was very sweet and consistent and so you get nervous with people coming in to change it, but so far we are doing all right," he smiles.

Outside of work, O'Quinn reveals he and his wife of 25 years recently decided to move from their long-time residence of Maryland to Hawaii for the duration of the series. "It's our only residence now. We decided to move because it was a part of our life that was coming to a close and the new part was beginning. That happens when your kids grow up and they leave the house and you begin to look at things in a different way. We were thinking about going out to LA, kind of as our only option, not because we totally wanted to be there. It made most sense so we could be together more and I wouldn't have to travel as much. Then *Lost* came along and we just decided to go to Hawaii. We didn't think of it as a permanent possibility until the show got healthy and then it was more likely. We're pretty happy right now!"

He also shares that it's been a change of scenery that has informed and changed both his take on Locke and his own well-being. "I think being in this environment makes it easier to drop into whatever it is your gonna drop into. It just adds a flavor to the soup that is your character. It definitely helps when you are here for a sustained period of time; it affects the racing speed of your mind. It's calmed me… I mean I was pretty calm, but it made me healthier in general. I walk a lot more and people here don't honk their horns, so that makes me healthier too," he laughs. "All those things are for a better state of mind."

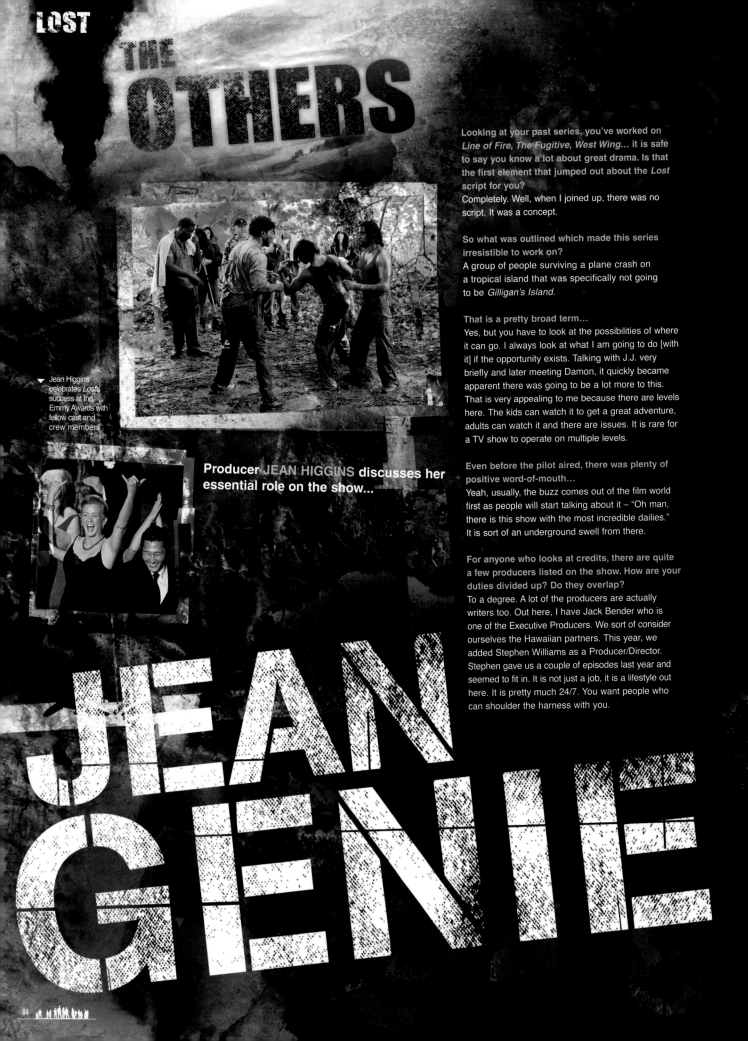

THE OTHERS

JEAN GENIE

Jean Higgins celebrates *Lost*'s success at the Emmy Awards with fellow cast and crew members

Producer JEAN HIGGINS discusses her essential role on the show...

Looking at your past series, you've worked on *Line of Fire, The Fugitive, West Wing*... **it is safe to say you know a lot about great drama. Is that the first element that jumped out about the** *Lost* **script for you?**
Completely. Well, when I joined up, there was no script. It was a concept.

So what was outlined which made this series irresistible to work on?
A group of people surviving a plane crash on a tropical island that was specifically not going to be *Gilligan's Island*.

That is a pretty broad term...
Yes, but you have to look at the possibilities of where it can go. I always look at what I am going to do [with it] if the opportunity exists. Talking with J.J. very briefly and later meeting Damon, it quickly became apparent there was going to be a lot more to this. That is very appealing to me because there are levels here. The kids can watch it to get a great adventure, adults can watch it and there are issues. It is rare for a TV show to operate on multiple levels.

Even before the pilot aired, there was plenty of positive word-of-mouth...
Yeah, usually, the buzz comes out of the film world first as people will start talking about it – "Oh man, there is this show with the most incredible dailies." It is sort of an underground swell from there.

For anyone who looks at credits, there are quite a few producers listed on the show. How are your duties divided up? Do they overlap?
To a degree. A lot of the producers are actually writers too. Out here, I have Jack Bender who is one of the Executive Producers. We sort of consider ourselves the Hawaiian partners. This year, we added Stephen Williams as a Producer/Director. Stephen gave us a couple of episodes last year and seemed to fit in. It is not just a job, it is a lifestyle out here. It is pretty much 24/7. You want people who can shoulder the harness with you.

How far into the water did you go for that raft sequence?
On that particular one, we were about a half a mile off shore. At that place, we were right over a reef so it was probably 14 feet deep.

Do you ever get a script and think, "How are we ever going to pull this off?"
Every script I get, my reaction as I sit down is, "That is great… how the hell are we going to do this?" And I will tell you that happens with *every* episode because they are so good and think so big! We sit down, start talking, and we figure out how to do it. If we weren't pushing the envelope every single week, we wouldn't have the show we do.

What were some of the other challenges last season?
Definitely the finale. There was a lot of water work at night. Hawaii is not a place that is conducive to water work – it is the Pacific Ocean and can be extremely rough and the current can be very strong out here. On any given day, the surf and the current can change anywhere on the island. We always have to have three alternatives in place. A lot of it is scheduling because the size and scope of the shows are so large and we only have eight dates to shoot each episode.

Harold Perrineau told *Lost Magazine* last issue that he can't swim…
True! The terror in Harold's eyes was absolutely real. To his credit, Harold is one of the nicest guys. He just jumped in and did it. Harold is an actor's actor. He is great. Josh had to do all the swimming with blue jeans on. Those really drag you down. The poor guy was exhausted!

Is there anything last season you regret not using more?
We are always trying to find and explore new areas of the island. The frustration is, being a television show, we have to do it in a certain period of time that is faster/shorter than a feature film. There are areas of the island that we are dying to use. Some of it is just a question of getting there.

BODY OF WORK

JEAN HIGGINS discusses the actors' embracing *Lost*'s physical aspects…

"They do as much as we will let them. We will always stop short of it becoming unsafe. Evangeline would do everything if we let her [laughs]! I say, 'But if you climbed a tree, accidentally fell out, you wouldn't be able to shoot the shot.' It is a very physical show and most of the actors would like to do more."

"The kids can watch it to get a great adventure, adults can watch it and there are issues. It is rare for a TV show to operate on multiple levels."

SIXTH SENSE

JEAN HIGGINS explains she had an intuition *Lost* was going to be a hit…

Quite a few guest directors tackle *Lost*. Do you have any words of wisdom before they land on the game field?
It is always a process getting visiting directors up to speed. I usually call them before they come out and say, "Okay, this is what it is like shooting our show. These are the kinds of clothes you need to bring and what the climate is like. And by the way, what my actors look like in front of the camera compared to the crew, me, and you…. we all look worse behind it [laughs]!"

The sand is soft and my crew have legs of iron. If you do a night shot, lighting the jungle is not the same as, "Lets go shoot at night at an intersection." Just making rain in the jungle where it rains the degree you want it to is a challenge. You can end up being up to your ankles in mud.

How much does weather affect filming?
Interestingly enough, very little. Last year, I changed the schedule twice for weather days. This year, I have done it once because Hurricane Kenneth was supposed to be right off the coast. Normally if it rains, we keep shooting anyway.

With the introduction of the tail-section survivors, *Lost* has multiple storylines this season instead of one island mystery and the flashbacks…
Yes, and it has brought more to the show. It has enriched it. With those two groups of people meeting up, it provides a whole new arena for conflict. It really does nothing but add to the show.

So far, season two's big reveal has been the hatch. Was it an ordeal coming up with the look for its interior?
The hatch went through a number of permutations as it was being built. There were a lot of discussions, a couple of redoes, and some alterations as it was so critical as to: "Where did it come from?" "Who built it?" "Why did it look this way?"

There have been some casualties on the island, namely Boone and Shannon. Does it take a toll on you doing those scenes?
Oh yeah, because you've grown to love those people. It is very real. Shooting Shannon's death recently was hard. The crew is very respectful. They give them their space.

Those scenes do pack an emotional punch…
They do and our show is about surviving on an island with very little. Those kind of things happen. If we were ever to take the edge off the fact that they are survivors and working at surviving, we lose the nucleus of the show. These people are discovering not only where they are, but who they are.

"Well, I knew it going in. Nobody really wanted to believe me. They had a little bit more trepidation, but I looked at my husband and said, 'We are going to become the new version of bi-coastal. Are you up for a minimum of three years of this?' And that was before I started shooting the pilot."

Are there certain aspects that make episodes favorites of yours?
Sometimes it is a favorite because of what we have managed to pull off – like faking Iraq in Honolulu. Sometimes it is because of the performances like when we hung Dominic [in episode #109, *All The Best Cowboys Have Daddy Issues*] – it was a killer and stunning moment. Sometimes it is just joy. Jack [Bender] and I were worried about the Sawyer/Kate plunge pool episode only because we thought it was lighter fare. We were delighted it came off so well and was so well received. It was one of the higher rated episodes. △

"Every script I get, my reaction as I sit down is, 'That is great… how the hell are we going to do this?' But if we weren't pushing the envelope every single week, we wouldn't have the show we do."

Thanks to the *Lost* Production Office, here are the original storyboards by Mike Swift of Kate's journey down the hatch shaft, with comparisons to how the shots actually turned out in the season two opener *Man of Science, Man of Faith*.

THE DESCENT

WIDE / LOCKE & KATE PEER DOWN HATCH

Kate and Locke peer inside, curious about what could be at the bottom of...

1

POV DOWN SHAFT

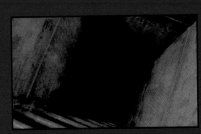

...the seemingly bottomless shaft

2

LOOKING UP SHAFT / LOCKE & KATE

We go to the reverse angle, and view the pair from inside the shaft

3

KATE'S POV.

ON KATE LOWERING HERSELF INTO SHAFT

WIDE / LOCKE

From Kate's point of view, we see her feet approach the edge of the ledge

4

Kate prepares herself before...

5

...Locke takes up the slack of the rope and begins to lower her into the shaft

6

3

25

ON KATE

ON KATE FROM BELOW

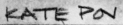

KATE POV   DOWN SHAFT

By torchlight, we watch Kate drift gradually lower and lower...

7

...with the camera staying behind Kate so we don't see what's beneath her

8

As you can see, there was originally a shot storyboarded from Kate's point of view, but this didn't end up in the final sequence

9

ON KATE CLOSE / PASSING END OF LADDER

10

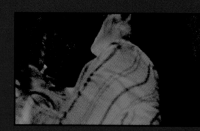

Kate continues her gradual descent...

ON LOCKE / HAND OVER HAND -

11

...and we cut between Kate's journey and Locke's task up-top of lowering her

12

This high angle storyboarded shot (left) showing the depth/narrowness of the shaft was also left on the cutting room floor

ON KATE CLOSE

ECU KATE

KATE "JOHN!"

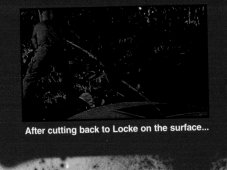

After cutting back to Locke on the surface...

13

...we jump back to Kate who is beginning to become concerned...

14

...that she is not alone, and that there is something down there with her

15

ON LOCKE WIPING/SCRATCHE HIS NOSE

KATE / OS
"JOHN!"

ROPE SLIPS -   cont.

WIDER, LOCKE STRUGGLES OFF
BALANCE,

Examine the storyboards very closely to
this next Locke sequence...

16

...compared to the simplified struggle with
the rope that ended up on screen...

17

...there was originally a very elaborate idea of
Locke scratching his nose and losing his grip
when the rope was yanked by Desmond...

18

7 LOCKE HANGS ON / PULLED ON HIS STOMACH!

19

At storyboard stage, poor Locke was dragged along...

20

...whereas the final version simply saw Locke struggle in a tug of war...

21

...with the focus being on Locke's grip on the rope gradually slipping...

The storyboards show a much longer struggle...

22

...with Locke pulled against his will towards the exposed outside wall of the hatch...

23

24

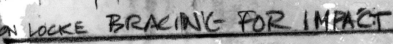
ON LOCKE BRACING FOR IMPACT

"...bracing for impact", whereas the episode kept the tension on the slipping rope

LOCKE SLAMS INTO SIDE OF HATCH

TUNNEL

cont.

KATE FALLS TO CAM / GRABS ROPE W/ BOTH HANDS DROPS LIGHT

LOCKE SLAMS INTO SIDE OF HATCH

25

Instead of colliding with the side of the hatch, Locke was pulled towards its opening...

26

...as we rejoin Kate inside to realize she is being pulled down...

27

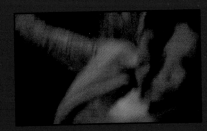

...as her torch drops and she screams

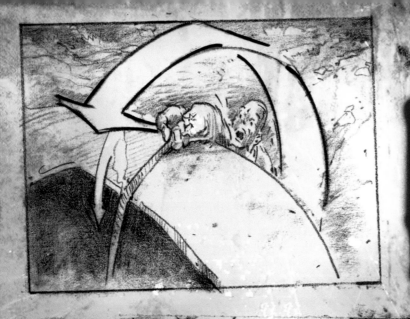

27

We can see how the show's team decided to cut to this idea of Locke bracing his feet against the edge...

HATCH EDGE

ELBOWS CATCH

28

...instead of having his elbows over the hatch edge

KATE F/G-SPLASH BELOW/FLASHLT. HITS BOTTOM-

29

KATE STOPS HERE

Kate jolts to a sudden stop...

LOCKE GETS TO HIS FEET

1½

KATE RISES SLOWLY TO CAM

KATE LOOKS DOWN

30

Locke uses all the strength he has to brace his legs against the hatch edge...

31

...and keep hold of Kate

32

She has come to a stop, but is terrified...

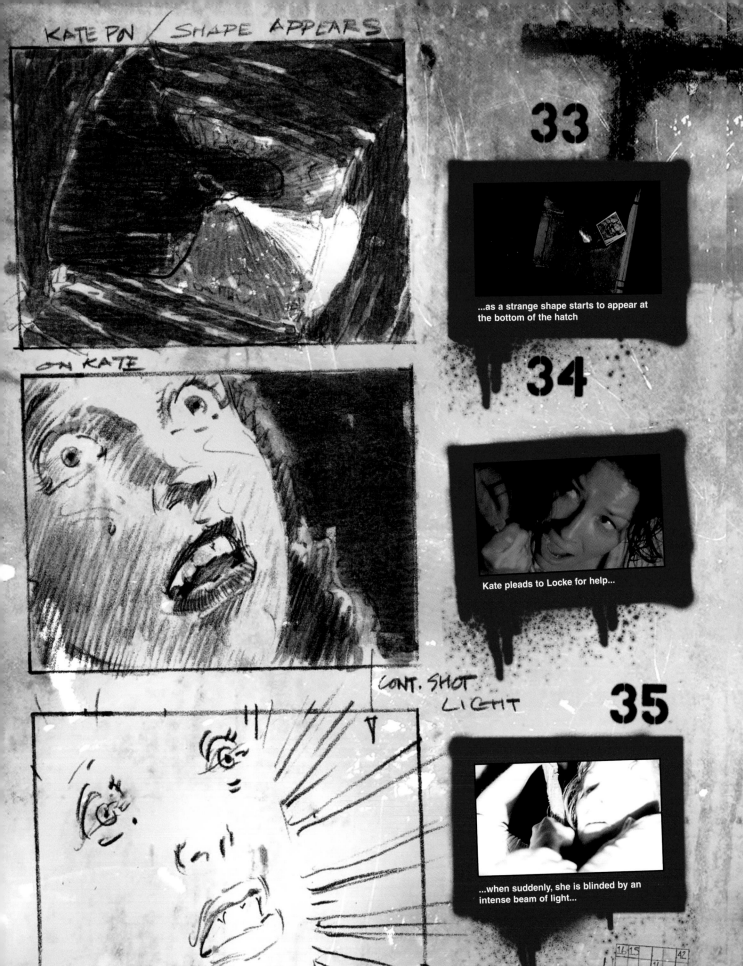

KATE POV / SHAPE APPEARS

ON KATE

CONT. SHOT
LIGHT

33

...as a strange shape starts to appear at the bottom of the hatch

34

Kate pleads to Locke for help...

35

...when suddenly, she is blinded by an intense beam of light...

WIDER / LIGHT BLOWS OUT FROM SHAFT

...a beam of light that reminds us of a shot from season one, as Locke, once again, gets consumed by it...

36

ON LOCKE CLOSE / TRYING TO PEER THRU LIGHT

...but this time the hatch door is open, and Locke peers inside past the light, terrified of what might have happened to Kate...

37

THIS TAKES US TO ROPE
GOING SLACK —

THE OTHERS

How did you end up as an Executive Producer for *Lost*?

I started working with J.J. in the middle of the first season of *Alias*. He was spending a lot of time in the Editors' Room and so wasn't able to spend the time he wanted to in the Writers' Room. Actually, he used to spend the full day in the Writers' Room and then would have to spend the full night in the Editors' Room [laughs]! So he asked me to come in and help him out – lock cuts [edits of the episodes] that were close to being locked, and so on.

I was in the feature film world at the time, doing development stuff, and toying with the idea of starting a videogame company, so I thought I would come in and do it for a couple of months and help J.J. out, and I ended up not leaving. We set up a project together, a feature film that we are producing at Universal, and when J.J. was working on his script for *Superman Lives*, I became his bounce board for that as well.

Going back a little, when season two of *Alias* rolled around, we had decided we were going to form a company together. We kept talking about it, but we were so swamped that we weren't able to get anything up and running. In the middle of season three of *Alias* when *Lost* came about, J.J. was also in the middle of doing *The Catch* [a pilot for a P.I. comedy that starred Greg Grunberg] and he got approached about the concept of 'people stuck on a deserted island.' The rest is history!

LIFE OF BRYAN

Stepping out of the dark place that is the Editors' Room, Executive Producer BRYAN BURK, discusses his role on the show.

...e of us knew Lost would catch ...e way that it did. As J.J. said ...on, 'At one point we felt like we ...in film school and we'd somehow ...ed to convince the faculty to let what we wanted..'

DESTINY'S CHILD

BRYAN BURK on why Locke's past, present and future are so involving…

"Well, I think Locke's back-story is the most developed and at the same time un-developed one. It's the one that makes you want to know what's going on with him. Is he good or evil, or a little of both? What does he know and what doesn't he know? Ultimately, what is his game plan? Does he even have a game plan? All of these things make him, to me, extremely intriguing. He has a great story."

...a day in the life of Bryan Burk like? ...*Lost* primarily. We have eight days to ...n episode, and as the footage and the ...are coming in, the editors are assem- ...the footage, as close to the script as ...e. When shooting is completed, the editor ...bles an 'editor's cut.' Whoever directed ...isode then comes in, and they usually ...r two or three days with the editor. Once ...e done their pass, that is the point where ...n. I see what we have, and I assess if ...ve any big problems which may involve ...ots, or new scenes, etc. ...xt our team of Writers and Producers ...heir notes and I sort through them, spend- ...urther four days in the editing room. I ...send the new cut to the studio and the ...rk and get all their final notes, and ...ss those that are addressable. Once I get

to what I believe to be the final cut, that gets shown to the Executive Producers for their final notes and then we lock the cut.

There is then about a week of sound design to do. With the sound effects – that is often where I come in, particularly if we're introducing an unknown "thing" or an important sound. Michael Giacchino, our genius composer, then scores it, after which we have about three days to do a mix. For the first day of the mix, they spend a whole day putting all the sounds in: the dialogue, the sound effects, the ambience, the music... everything. They spend the next day smoothing it all out and adjusting the levels as best as they can in one day. At the end of that second night, I go in and see what they have and give them my notes. The final third day is the 'fixer day,' – where we do our best to make it sound like a feature film.

...Hurley... **which was always a funny story - also has a really dark side to it. The idea that he'd been in this mental hospital before... what was he doing there?"**

L to R: Dan Wallin (Recording Engineer) and Michael Giacchino (Composer) work on the latest *Lost* score

SURFACE

Lost has barely started revealing the characters' histories, BRYAN BURK reveals...

"What I'm excited about, is that as well as Locke, *all* the other characters have the same complexities. So far, we really have only scratched the surface as to who they are, and who they claim to be. For example, Hurley's story – which is a funny story – also has a really dark side to it. The idea that he'd been in a mental hospital before... what was he doing there? There are a lot of characters that we don't know about yet. What we think we know about them is really only the tip of the iceberg."

What aspects of a show like Lost really appeal to you?
Originally, what I was always excited about, which made it different from most TV shows, is that there are always three elements at play on the show. Man against nature, man against man. And man against the unknown. None of us knew *Lost* would catch on the way that it did. As J.J. said early on, "At one point we felt like we were in film school and we'd somehow managed to convince the faculty to let us do what we wanted." That's exactly what it's like. It feels like you're in college again and all those crazy ideas that you have that you want to do, and all those movies that inspire you, it's like, "Hey, they're letting us do it!" We've been able to create a show that has inspiration from all the films, TV shows, books and videogames we've always loved – but in its own way, it's really not like anything else.

You guys are all fans of Twin Peaks aren't you?
For me, *Twin Peaks* was as good as television gets. David Lynch is a genius. Early on, when we were conceiving *Lost*, we had many discussions with regard to how Lynch and Mark Frost were able to pull off *Twin Peaks*. ⚠

THE PSALM
BEFORE THE STORM

Getting to be a guest director for *Lost* is one thing...
bagging Mr. Eko's visceral back-story and the first proper
showing of the 'monster' is a dream gig. Director of season
two's *The 23rd Psalm*, MATT EARL BEESLEY, provides an
exclusive insight into shooting the pivotal episode...

Flashbacks

to Africa, more personal turmoil between the island survivors and a jaw-dropping, extended view of the oft heard but never seen 'monster' were just some of the elements that made up the stunning 10th episode of this season, *The 23rd Psalm*. True to the *Lost* format, those engaging elements were woven together to create an even bigger story that gave audiences their first glimpse into the mysterious past of the Tailie man of faith, Mr. Eko (Adewale Akinnuoye-Agbaje). With exotic locations to be built, complex visual effects shots to be blocked and a host of emotional character moments, *The 23rd Psalm* was an especially daunting episode to bring to life, but that didn't faze veteran director Matt Earl Beesley.

Despite being his first time helming an episode for *Lost*, Beesley says he was more than ready for the task, with only one goal in mind when he stepped off the plane in Oahu, Hawaii. "My challenge was that I just didn't want to mess it up!" Beesley jokes.

No chance of that considering Beesley's respected career as an assistant director for films like *Big Trouble in Little China*, *Christmas Vacation* and *Chain Reaction*. It's a career that had its roots in his childhood love of movies. "It's funny," Beesley reflects. "It's the only thing I've ever wanted to do. It's weird. When I was a kid, all my friends would go out and hang out and party. What would I do? I'd go to a movie. I'd be watching movies with my dad. I still remember going to triple bills with my dad at the drive-in. So I went to film school at SMU (Southern Methodist University) at Texas. I gradated with a Bachelors of Fine Arts degree and started working for a little independent film company in Dallas. We got these opportunities to go to Europe and do these movies. All the assistant directors I met over there were directors in training, so I figured I'd move to Los Angeles and become an assistant director and work my way up to being a director. In LA, it doesn't work that way. If you are an assistant director, you end up becoming a producer or a production manager, so I had to work my way back through the process. I started directing a lot of second unit [sequences] and my biggest credit was second unit directing *Braveheart*. It got me going and a lot of directors I worked with kept letting me go off to direct second unit, so slowly but surely I worked my way into directing full time, and wound up in television, where I love to be!"

In recent years, Beesley has directed episodes of *Prison Break*, *CSI* and *Law & Order*, but *Lost* has been on his radar since the first season. "I'd been a big fan of the show, so I watched every episode last season. On *Lost*, my mentor on the show is a guy named Jack Bender [Executive Producer]. I've known him since I was a grad out of film school. He's the one that pulled me into the ranks of doing this episode. He actually booked me on an episode for the first season and then they had a schedule shift. When they shifted, I was already booked on another show. We tried to arrange it so I could get out of my commitment but it turned out that it didn't work out, so I wound up not getting to do one the first season. He promised me one for this season and sure enough, he gave me a really good one to do."

The 23rd Psalm gave Beesley a little bit of everything to direct, from complex location flashbacks to intimate character moments. In prepping for the episode, Beesley says his intent was to stay true to the small moments of the show. "I wanted each scene to feel real. What's so great about the show is that it's such a wild ride that these characters go through, the different elements of the island, the struggles there and all their back stories. The characters are set up so strongly, that you believe they are real, so when they are going through these really bizarre situations, you buy into it!"

Sure, Hawaii is beautiful, but it's beautiful plus you are up to your ankles in mud and it's pouring down rain when you are trying to finish a scene and there are bugs flying all around you and then the sun comes out and the lighting doesn't match (laughs)!

Arriving on the island for production, Beesley says it was a whirlwind from day one. "Because of my work schedule, I didn't get the opportunity to go out ahead of time and observe. I literally got off the plane and hit the ground running. I felt like I was familiar with, definitely, the format and definitely, the characters and what they were trying to achieve. But I must say, the actual experience itself was one of the most intense shows I've ever done. Talk about working with the elements! The warriors on that show are both the cast and the crew. They get in there and go, "OK, these are the cards that are dealt… we're going to do the best we can." You're in a situation where you are halfway through a scene and it starts pouring down rain, so you have to commit to shooting in the rain or waiting it out. Literally, working in the jungle, it's harsh conditions. You think, 'Oh great – it's Hawaii!' Sure, it's beautiful, but it's beautiful *plus* you are up to your ankles in mud and it's pouring down rain when you are trying to finish a scene and there are bugs flying all around you and then the sun comes out and the lighting doesn't match!" he laughs. "That cast and crew are great under some pretty tricky conditions."

Despite all of that to contend with, Beesley says it was still smooth sailing because of the strength of the script. "First of all, the coolest thing about the show is that the scripts are so dead on. Coming in as a guest director, Damon [Lindelof] and Jack [Bender] and all of them gave me what I consider a gift. They gave me such a great groundwork of a script. To be able to tell the back-story of Eko was amazing. I felt thrilled to have that as my story. I also had such a great support system, with meeting after meeting going through the script page-by-page, scene-by-scene making sure everybody was on the same page with the story. Then getting to work with that cast! Those actors over there, they really do care about cranking out the best storytelling they can. All of them are so true to their characters that it's a joy."

Especially impressive to Beelsey was his leading man of the episode, Adewale Akinnuoye-Agbaje. The duo bonded over the fact that this episode afforded both men their first times to shine on the show and their collaborative connection was a strong foundation for them both. "Adewale is such an intense and fantastic actor," the director enthuses. "When I first got the script, I was already interested and intrigued by his character. I was like the audience thinking, 'What's the story with this guy?' Eko does a really good job about listening to the other characters. You can tell he thinks about his response before he just blurts something out. He's very studied in his response, just like Adewale chooses to have those pauses before he actually speaks. He is a very methodical person. One of the first things I did in Hawaii was to sit down with Adewale and have a tone meeting to talk about the character and what he thought about the character and why this was an important story."

With much of Eko's flashback story referring back to his life in Africa, Beelsey and his team had the particular challenge of bringing the plains to life in the much more tropical environment of Hawaii. With the help of locations and the other *Lost* production departments, they were able to create a credible Nigerian town right on Oahu.

"One of the things we found, which was a centerpiece for Nigeria, was an old, abandoned sugar factory," Beesley relates. "I remembered what you always hear about in Africa is that they pump all this money into the economy to build these factories and they don't work out and they abandon them. So we found this old factory and with the help of the fantastic set decorator and costume designer, we were able to build this Nigerian market.

What I thought was important, was that Eko would clearly challenge the 'monster' ... Adewale is so grounded in that character and believes so strongly in the convictions of Eko, that I just described what he was seeing, and he tuned right into that.

"Another challenge is that there aren't a lot of African Americans in Hawaii," he continues. "So what casting did was go to military bases and they found wives and kids of soldiers and actual military personnel and asked if they wanted to be in a *Lost* episode. We had them come down and dressed them up and away we went!"

Of course, the one scene that had audiences stunned into silence was the shocking visual introduction of the 'monster,' last glimpsed at the end of season one as a barely-there, wispy trail of smoke. As Eko and Charlie trek alone in the jungle, the 'monster' appears again, only this time much more dramatically, as it confronts Eko in the shape of a menacing black cloud of organized ether. Thrilled at being able to show the 'monster' in his episode, Beesley details the sequence was carefully crafted for maximum effect. "We storyboarded the sequence out and we had several meetings with Carlton [Cuse] Damon [Lindelof], Bryan Burk the post-production and special effects guys, and Jack [Bender] just to make sure we all knew what it was we were going for. It was about halfway through the shoot that we shot that sequence. I had a good working relationship with Adewale by that point, so I was able to describe what it was that he was seeing. What I thought was important, was that he, as a character, would clearly challenge the 'monster,' which had not happened before. I think that Adewale is so grounded in that character and believes so strongly in the convictions of Eko, that I just described what he was seeing and he tuned right into that."

SOMETHING PERSONAL

Director MATT EARL BEESLEY explains why the setting of *The 23rd Psalm* meant a lot to him…

"I'm very involved with an organization that tries to get relief to Africa. I was in Romania years ago doing a movie and I was reading the International Herald Tribune, which gives the news a more international flavor. I started to see the world from a different perspective. You start reading articles about landmines and people trying to make a difference. So I started doing research about organizations that try to make a difference with children. Just by doing that I found this British charity called War Child [www.warchild.org]. They go and they try to make a difference by pulling out these kids in these war torn situations and trying to give them a safe haven. I felt like I got a gift with this script [*The 23rd Psalm*] because this is something I am already passionate about."

The finished sequence was a visual effects highlight for the series, but Beesley says the true excitement for him was what was happening with Eko and Charlie. "I think they did a great job with the visual effects, but the emotional impact of what was going on for those characters was what made it real to me. In the story, there is a connection between those two guys. The different journeys and backgrounds of those men thrown out into the jungle with different agendas, yet they are still trying to find each other within that setting. And the fact that we had Dominic 40 feet up in the air in a tree was quite the challenge also," he laughs, detailing Charlie's climb.

"We found this tree and asked him what he thought and he goes, "Sure, I'm game." I don't think he had the best time, but that's also what made it real. We brought him up there in a cherry picker and strapped him in to make sure that he was secure, but even with that there was no net below him. I was struggling so hard to make sure that we got enough angles to actually show that he was up there. You can fake that pretty easily, but I thought it was much more graphic and haunting situation to put Dom up in the tree."

The 23rd Psalm struck an immediate cord with audiences and personally for Beesley, it was everything he could have hoped for on his first adventure with *Lost*. "It was a really terrific script and as a filmmaker it's so important to have something that starts on the page and has an emotional impact. It's funny. It is entertainment and it's a TV show, but I think it touches people emotionally."

Asked if he will return to the island soon, Beesley enthusiastically shares, "I really want to come back this season, but the way my schedule worked out, I don't think it's going to be possible. But they already told me, I'll be back next season and I can't wait!"

EVERYBODY LOVES HURLEY

4 8 15 16 23 42

Between hiding tubs of Dharma Ranch Dressing, working his charm on Libby and calling his fellow survivors "Dude," Hurley keeps his friends' sanity intact. JORGE GARCIA talks about playing the number-centric character, and how he enjoys the laughs off-screen as much as on it...

"I get messages from people on The Fuselage who keep telling me they are using the numbers to play the lottery and I keep writing back, 'Stop it! The numbers are bad!'"

When

creators J.J. Abrams and Damon Lindelof were carefully crafting the survivors for their series *Lost*, it was doubtful they could have predicted how their specific visions would evolve. For instance, Dr. Jack Shephard was originally supposed to die in the pilot before living on to emerge as the island's leader. The aging rock star druggie Charlie Pace was dipped into the fountain of youth for a fresh perspective. Similarly, the mellow and endearing Hugo "Hurley" Reyes was transformed before actor Jorge Garcia's eyes. "I remember seeing a description of Hurley and it was a little ambiguous but one of the things they had was a red shirt," recalls Garcia. "I didn't realize what that meant exactly but he seemed like a guy they weren't planning on sticking around too long as far as the series goes. There had been descriptions of him being a redneck around his 50s. He's totally different in the same way Sawyer was a New York con man. They start with ideas but were willing to change them once they got inspired by certain actors that came in."

That was certainly the case with Garcia when they recognized his potential from his guest-starring stint on an acclaimed comedy series. "I had done this episode of *Curb Your Enthusiasm* that had just aired," explains Garcia. "They called me in and at the time, they didn't have any sides for me to read but I think I was already being considered for Hurley. Since they didn't have any sides, I had to read for Sawyer and that was my first meeting with the producers. Then I actually tested when they had sides for Hurley but even then, I hadn't read a full script. I didn't get one until I booked the job."

Trapped on a mysterious island after their flight crash-landed, *Lost* unveils bits and pieces of its characters through flashbacks while dealing with present day pandemonium. Unfortunately, Garcia had to patiently wait until the 18th episode before the spotlight shifted to Hurley, and by then, he was already connecting the dots about his alter ego's baggage. "They did start dropping clues which I started following around," explains Garcia. "When they added the line of me owing Walt a lot of money, Hurley answered 'You'll get it!' Stuff like that presented clues along the way. But that is part of doing *Lost* – working with the information you have, filling in your own blanks, and then sometimes getting contradictory information later. I enjoy that side of *Lost* because it is very human to behave in a different way than you would have expected in the same situation. That works for the show."

Numbers featured Hurley striking it rich with a record $156 million jackpot, nearly missing his flight, and the bombshell that he had spent some quality time in a sanitarium. "Because I had learned that Hurley was going to be a lottery winner and was going to be rich, what I was waiting on was the *Twilight Zone* moment later where you find the numbers on the hatch," says Garcia. "That was a big deal for me. Also finding out he was in a mental institution at some point was an added bonus. It is interesting and still an untapped part of Hurley's back-story that we don't know about. What put him there?"

Perhaps the growing evidence that his lottery numbers – 4, 8, 15, 16, 23, and 42 – are jinxed is what pushed him over the deep end? After all, his grandpa unexpectedly dropped dead, his mother snapped her ankle and witnessed her luxurious home ignite, and later, Oceanic Airlines Flight 815 plunged from the sky with Hurley onboard. So what does it all mean? "Since Hurley is a very close friend of mine, I'm going to go with him in his belief that the numbers are cursed even though no one else thinks they are," offers Garcia. "I get messages from people on The Fuselage who keep telling me they are using the numbers to play the lottery and I keep writing back, 'Stop it! The numbers are bad!' I don't know if we are ever going to know what they mean but they have some purpose at the moment. They do a job. Sure, I'd love for something to come down that puts all those number pieces together and the longer you wait, the higher the anticipation. We'll see if it pays off or not."

CONVENTIONAL

JORGE GARCIA on getting up, close, and personal with the fans…

"Personally, fans are why we have the kinds of jobs we do. They are the ones who give us the audience, the ratings for the show. The fact they help keep it going by continuing to talk about it beyond Thursday morning, analyzing it… I think it is awesome. I wasn't so sure about conventions but it gives fans an opportunity to come up with some face time with me. I had fans who have come up to me and said, 'Please keep doing these conventions' because they like the chance to meet us. I've used this quote a lot but it's true when Terry [O'Quinn] said, 'There's something really cool about the fact that all you have to do is show up sometimes and you make someone's day.'"

HURLEY LINGO

JORGE GARCIA discusses two memorable words from Hurley's laid back vocabulary…

"It is so funny because in that 'I'm spry' moment in *Numbers*, there was a previous episode where 'I'm spry' was first used but didn't make the cut. That is why they brought it back. In the episode where they have to kill the Marshal, Jack is just standing there and all of a sudden, I show up next to him and startle him for a second. He's like, 'Where did you come from? I didn't even hear you show up.' And Hurley's like, 'I'm spry.' That was our favorite moment. We were cracking up doing that particular scene and then it didn't make the show. We were disappointed but it was good that it actually came back."

That episode also saw a frustrated Hurley get intense and step outside his easy-going persona by demanding some "freaking answers" from "French chick," Danielle. "I definitely want to do more moments like that. I get a lot of comments about Hurley's strong realism and a lot of people do focus on it. I do want to be true to that. It is great because I get to show off a little bit of what I can do as an actor. I'm kind of that way too. I'm very much like a Taurus by nature. It takes a lot of push to take them over the edge but when it happens, it is a time when you have to watch out. And you have to push a lot before you get there."

Even as he rested on a booby trap pressure trigger, Hurley remained unnaturally calm and zoomed out of there, like it was no big deal. "About Hurley flying by the seat of his pants, well the situation in *Numbers* had that more of a man-on-a-mission quality to it," explains Garcia. "Here, he finally got to step in the direction of what these numbers might mean to him. Still, I think what was important was to keep going in his quest. He doesn't take the time to worry about what might happen and makes the move. So far, he's been alright though."

Throughout the series, Garcia has welcomed his fair share of physical activity, from trudging though the mud and rain to being chased by the 'monster.' "From the pilot where I had to run from the plane wing that came crashing down and exploded behind me, I knew this was going to involve stuff way beyond anything I'd be doing in my acting career," reflects Garcia. "I enjoyed *Numbers* when someone started getting shot at and just running through the jungle into the fall I had to do. Besides the pilot, that fall was my first stunt once we were an official series. I was really happy with the fall. Mike Vendrell, our stunt coordinator, said it was awesome. It earned me a Hawaii Stunt Connection T-shirt for doing my own stunt… although I totally missed the pad. I basically face planted with my arms and face in the mud."

Despite being strangers stuck on a deserted island, the survivors have formed their own alliances and friendships and for Hurley, that means gaining a best friend in Charlie. "Charlie and Hurley are the closest equivalent to a couple of college kids hanging around," states Garcia. "The whole scene we recently did where we are listening to records… that kind of stuff I just love. And I think it is going to get even more so as it goes on. It has been pretty consistent. I guess we have had some rifts but we come back together very strongly."

After Charlie's desperate attempt for attention and being ostracized by his peers, he probably needs Hurley now more than ever. "Yeah, but even Hurley turned away a bit," notes Garcia. "Charlie is kind of endangering the baby and definitely seemed out of character. They will come back together for sure though."

With a lot of his scenes interacting with Jack and Charlie, Garcia is ecstatic about exploring those dynamics with fellow actors Matthew Fox and Dominic Monaghan. "It is fantastic!" says Garcia. "Dom and I are very good friends and he basically lives around the corner. If I'm walking to the beach, I have to pass his house, which is always worth a knock on the door to see if he's around for a swim or whatever. It is a joy when you look forward to your scenes that you are coming in to do at work.

"Foxy and I sometimes have a problem keeping a straight face working with each other. There won't even be much going on. It happens even if they are scenes where we don't actually speak and just share looks. We did a scene where Dr. Artz tells us when we were supposed to leave and he turns to say, 'Yesterday.' There's that moment right before the commercial break where there is silence and you see eyes exchange glances. You look to Michael, to Sawyer, to Jack, and the fact that we end on each other makes us laugh and blows the moment. Foxy says, 'I can't even look at you!' because after two takes, he can't do it. The rest of the takes we didn't laugh, and the last take… we think maybe we can do it, but no, we didn't. We started cracking up again."

Apparently Garcia and Fox's antics aren't only reserved for in front of the camera either. "Foxy and I had some great moments in the finale we were shooting last year," reveals Garcia. "There was a lot of mud and rain and a lot of stuff to deal with, like Locke getting dragged down a hole. Those were some really rough days, and also times when you want to pick everyone up and get them moving with a good attitude. So near the end of that season, Matt poured water on my pants and that became a thing between us. It was 'getting the other person's pants wet in different ways' – like squirting them with a spray bottle in the crotch. We started doing that back and forth, where one person does it, and then it is the other person's turn. On one of the last days, I finished before he did so I put ice cubes in the pockets of his *real* pants, in the hope they would melt [once he'd finished shooting]. I was thinking, 'Wow! This is a great master evil plan.' Then I get a call from Foxy saying, 'You really crossed the line there. I've always attacked wardrobe… and here you went after civilian clothes [laughs]! It is going to happen… you are not going to know when, but I already know what I'm going to do to get you back.' He hasn't done it yet and now I'm thinking maybe that might be his method of keeping me on edge. Either that or he's completely forgotten."

In typical *Lost* fashion, the creative team has added turbulence in season two by introducing some new blood, most notably Ana Lucia, Libby, and Mr. Eko. The three characters are part of the Tailies, a group of survivors from the doomed flight and their presence meant yet another storyline was being woven into the series. "When we started [season two], it was like working on two different shows," recalls Garcia. "We would work on completely different days than the Tailies did because they worked in different locations. We would see episodes and it was like a whole other group of people. As they started getting closer and closer to reaching our camp, their work days got closer too. We came off doing our beach scenes and they were about to start on their scenes and we were walking around saying to Harold [Perrineau] and Daniel [Dae Kim], 'Wow! We missed you guys! It is like you are doing a whole different project.' But I enjoyed it very much. We had this natural chemistry from everyone who did season one. In many ways, like the premise of the show, it is almost like we survived something as a group and bonded because of it. Now we have new Tailies, new chemistries to form, and have to figure out what our relationships are going to be. It is great as an actor to have to stay on your toes and keep getting new people to work with."

With Hurley's long stares and attempts at conversation, there now seems to be a spark flaring between him and Libby. "I'm not sure how it is going to progress yet," says Garcia about the budding romance. "It actually went a little further but that part didn't make it because of time: Hurley asks Libby if she'd like to take a walk, which would be the island's equivalent of a date, and it showed us actually walking. It is an aspect you don't always get to play, especially in an island adventure. It will be fun, but they are slow-playing it. They could totally pick that up if they wanted to and go a lot faster," he chuckles.

Once the mysterious hatch was blown open, Hurley quickly discovered being placed in charge of the food reserves was no picnic. However, once again, he showed his good heart by distributing the rations among everyone. "There was a lot of stuff for the audience to fill in but it did seem like it was a reaction to how he was treated after winning the lottery back home, this time with food instead of money," confirms Garcia. "It is whatever was of value at the time. The whole time he is going through the rant is when you see how his best buddy reacts to him being the winner in the lottery. I think there is still more to be revealed. It did seem somehow that the lottery ended his friendship back in his previous life. That episode probably caused the main rift he had with Charlie too when he knew Hurley had food and he couldn't give it up."

If only everyone on the island looked at the bigger picture. Although Sawyer has ruffled plenty of feathers, besides nicknames, Hurley has stayed off his radar until now. "Sawyer is an interesting guy," muses Garcia. "He's a con man, so the character really is an actor. You know that movie *House of Games* where they say, 'You are a confidence man not because people put their confidence in you but because you put your confidence in them.' So he's good at making a spiel that he needs us in many ways. He's got this tough thing but when he needs to work an angle, he has a problem and asks for my help. He has a problem with another one of the island's animals that shows up. Essentially, in a blackmail kind of way, he convinces Hurley to help him resolve his problem because he's desperate. Sawyer doesn't completely change and become Hurley's friend in the end either. You can never fully trust him and when you do, you get left hanging."

HEY DUDE!

JORGE GARCIA on improvising beyond the occassional extra "dude"…

"I've ad-libbed a couple of times over the course of the show. I did one where they were delaying saying, 'Cut!' In the episode where Hurley does the census, there's a moment where I ask Locke, 'What was the purpose of this trip?' and he says, 'Looking for something and I might find it.' Then he says 'No, it found me' or has some weird cryptic answer. I'm supposed to then go chase down one of our background people and I added the line, 'Look, I know I already talked to you but I wanted to get away from that guy.' Knowing the mic was on and they hadn't said 'cut,' I did that line in one take and it ended up being the one they used. Then another time, me and Dom do a little bit of chatter during the first golf game."

> "Charlie and Hurley are the closest equivalent to a couple of college kids hanging around. The whole scene we recently did where we are listening to records... that kind of stuff I just love."

In the upcoming Hurley-centric episode, the former fast food employee re-visits what exactly landed him in the nuthouse. "That has been the biggest unanswered question as far as Hurley goes, so it is about time!" says Garcia. "I was really hoping that would be part of my first flashback."

Many *Lost* cast members have professed being in the dark concerning plot details but when asked about a 'special friend' that plays a significant role in that storyline, it is obvious Garcia actually isn't faking when he says he doesn't know... "Ohhhh...you mean *Phil*?" he inquires. "Oh man. It is funny because we get scripts after casting. I have friends in LA who sometimes call me about parts and I'm like 'I have no idea what script you are talking about.' Someone asked me about a character named Phil and I was like, 'What episode he is supposed to be in?' He said the 18th, which is my episode, so now I'm wondering. Cool."

Hurley has been involved with the island threats as well as interacting with the castaways, and Garcia notes, "The scenes with Jin where he tried to give him an urchin to the moment he peed on my foot are my favorites. I like the relationship with Jin. Even though Jin pushes him away a lot, Hurley still goes out of his way to make friends. Same thing when Jin goes golfing with the rocks. I'm just trying to see how he's doing. I like that a lot. I like being part of the people who go on treks, although there is a bigger risk of not making it back."

For the record, it has been rumored that the *Lost* writers enjoy Hurley too much to ever send him with a one way ticket to join deceased step-siblings Boone and Shannon. "Yeah, that is great to hear," chuckles Garcia about being untouchable. "I'll say that much. It is crazy here. There are people who disappear for a long time too. You can do more than just kill somebody off. It is a fun ride and I enjoy doing it but it is a dangerous, dangerous island we all live on and we all know it."

Nevertheless, there would be quite an uproar if Hurley ever disappeared. As the loveable teddy bear type, devoted female fans have been mailing in love letters and propositioning Garcia with marriage. Understandably, he isn't quite ready to embrace that heartthrob status quite yet. "I don't even think about it," admits Garcia. "What makes Hurley so sexy? I don't know. I'd like to see the kind of stuff Josh has been getting before we look at that aspect [laughs]! It is funny and usually it is joking. Usually it is, 'Hey, single. LOL snicker snicker.' Stuff like that is usually what I get. Hurley is the 'Awww' guy, the guy that makes you go 'Awww...Look at that. Awww...' Sometimes 'Awww' guys get a lot of girl attention. Sawyer gets the, 'Ooooo... we don't know about him' kind of attraction thing."

Regardless, as Garcia's popularity skyrockets and *Lost* continues to be a ratings blockbuster, it is fame that is not an easy concept to grasp. The week before this interview, Garcia anxiously sat in the audience and vividly recalls what raced through his mind when *Lost* was named as Outstanding Performance by an Ensemble in a Drama Series at the 2006 SAG Awards.

"Yeahhh!" exclaims Garcia, "That is pretty much how it goes. Every time I'm surprised. Even when we're going through the red carpet treatment, I think at the Emmys, people were saying we were the odds on favorite for it and I had no idea we were coming in as the favorite. So much happens from the time people vote to things that go on, you never really know until you hear your name read. I get surprised every time we win something."

THE OTHERS

SHOOTING PEOPLE

Director of Photography LARRY FONG is lured out of hiding to discuss his role on the show...

Versatility

and talent must be the key to Director of Photography Larry Fong's success. Having attended the Art Centre of Design in Pasadena, he began studying photography before switching majors to film. Soon after graduation, he cut his teeth doing music videos, most notably REM's 'Losing My Religion,' then commercials, television, and movies. In essence, Fong has done it all.

"My duties are to visually capture on film the vision of the director so that involves lighting, composition, assembly of the crew, blocking shots, designing camera moves, choosing equipment and lenses," he explains. "Also with big pictures, giving a project an overall look that best tells the story."

Before *Lost*, Fong hadn't ventured into the world of serialized television but he had a personal connection that came knocking on his door. "J.J. Abrams called me," reveals Fong. "I knew him from way back before either of us did what we do. We've only collaborated once before on a TV commercial but it is safe to say we are pretty good friends. I was doing mostly the commercial route and of course he was doing television. He gave me a call and it sounded like a great project but no matter what the project was, I probably would have said yes."

Involved since the planning stages, Fong had some creative input into the tone and mood of the series. "J.J. and I did the usual thing which is sit down and watch movies of things you think might be a springboard to the look," says Fong. "We looked at so many things and neither of us liked anything we saw but it provides a point of departure for what we want to do. J.J. is pretty busy so we only saw a few seconds of every movie. Because he's so busy, I wouldn't say we had a ton of prep time but thank God we are friends because he was able to convey in a short amount of time what he wanted. I was able to understand what he wanted so there wasn't anything specific going on other than he wanted their plane to look huge and foreboding on the beach, he wanted the crash to be terrifying, and the island to take on its own sense of personality. Besides that, I think he said, 'Make it look really good.' Believe it or not, that is a cinematographer's dream because so often you want to be quick and cheap. When someone that powerful says it has to look good, that is fantastic."

Even before the cast settled in Hawaii, scouting for locations was an important task that presented some unexpected obstacles. "The greatest thing about Oahu is that there is paradise, island, and jungle but also civilization," offers Fong. "As you know, the flashbacks all take place in civilization so we've had to make Honolulu look like Iraq, Japan, Los Angeles, and New York. That took a lot of creative location scouting but we did go to Hawaii several times before shooting. At least for the pilot, the hardest part was trying to find beach where we could close off and not have people snorkeling while we were shooting. They found this beach way at the end of the island at the end of the highway. Still, the road was there at the edge of the plane covered by sand and occasionally we stopped to let cars go through. It was literally 20 feet away. We were also near an airport so every five takes or so we'd have to cut because there were guys jumping out with parachutes right above our heads. There was a glider that would come by every couple of hours and bug us…'Cut!'"

NEW PILOT REUNION

LARRY FONG recently completed the TV pilot *Secrets of a Small Town* that reunited him with John Terry who plays Jack's father, Dr. Christian Shephard…

"It was crazy," chuckles Fong. "All of a sudden, I see John walk in and I'm like, 'What the hell are you doing here?' It was great hanging with him and talking about old times and the crew because he was traveling back and forth. Of course, he's the evil rich guy in the town whose daughter is murdered. It could really be great. I was just happy to be shooting real people in real houses instead of naked Greek men on a mountain or people being chased by a 'monster' in the jungle. That was one of the reasons I took it. Back to reality."

Another exotic location that periodically pops up is Australia. The first episode featured Kate behind the wheel of a truck in the land Down Under, a place where you drive on the opposite side of the road. "That's not such a big deal on the set but we couldn't get any cars that had steering wheels on the wrong side for certain scenes so we shot everything and reversed the film," explains Fong. "We had to put jewelry on the other side of her; for the guy who had a fake arm we had to put the fake arm on the other arm. Everybody was so confused but all I did on the video monitor, was flip a switch and it reverses it. It wasn't that hard and it is funny how the simplest solutions come out."

" The flashbacks all take place in civilization so we've had to make Honolulu look like Iraq, Japan, Los Angeles, and New York. That took a lot of creative location scouting. "

The two-part series premiere packed a wallop with its realistic plane crash and Fong recalls the discussions and direction that went into that unforgettable sequence. "It was interesting because we had the whole set up and J.J. is very prepared," he says. "He draws storyboards in advance but what is amazing about him is he can improvise and think on his feet. With that shot, we only kind of had an idea how it was going to work. We just walked around in circles until we collaboratively threw out ideas. Matthew Fox comes out, just sees this beautiful ocean so we went around the corner where he couldn't really see the airplane. That led to a long walk, which is his discovery of paradise, then to weirdness, to screaming. What is cool about that is there is no point of view so he sees what is going on before we do. You slowly start to hear the sound, see the wreckage, and only in the end do you see the plane in the background. That is the genius because people realize at different times what is going on. That is why it was so powerful."

Of course, part of *Lost*'s magic is it combines the island adventure with intriguing flashbacks and both segments have a distinct look. "That was fun," says Fong about creating that uniqueness. "The way I approach cinematography is you have to light the environment, mood, and what is in front of the camera dictates how you are going to do it. If you have a shadowy jungle, you don't pour tons of light on the person and make it look like somewhere else. You let the beach dictate the look: natural and non-lit, but nothing could be further from the truth. If you went to the beach and turned the camera on, well if they are front lit, they are going to be blown out. If they are back-lit, you won't see enough of them. In the jungle, there's not enough light to shoot naturally but when you start putting lights in there, if there is too much, it looks fake. Of course, you can't always put the light exactly where you want because there are vines and trees in the way but you do your best."

AWARD RECOGNITION

LARRY FONG on being nominated for an American Society of Cinematographers Award for the *Lost* pilot…

"That was great and felt really good, it was definitely an honor. Some people go through a lifetime without getting that kind of nomination. I was pretty proud because of it and on TV it is always kind of hectic. J.J. gave us the freedom to really do cool stuff and take the time to do epic shots. There is a lot of handheld shots but there are also a lot of really nice composed dolly moves and interesting stuff. That is a lot of trouble and time so to make that a priority in a TV show… and there's more than just the beach [too]. There is the interior of the airplane, when they go up and it is raining inside the cockpit which I conceived as a haunted house – a dark and spooky thing."

"The flashbacks are cool because you really get to play," he continues. "Like in Iraq, we make it look really yellowy, green, hot, dusty, and hard light. You do that through color, quality of light, and lensing. Then when we did Korea, it is a whole other look again. There can be several ways to go when you are on a set so you get more choices with the flashback. Michael Bonvillain, the other Director of Photography when I was doing it, has different approaches and I would go, 'Wow! That is cool! I wouldn't have done that.' But he had a different story and it worked perfectly for what he was doing. Michael would do a lot of Jack's flashbacks which I never did."

With a 'monster,' polar bears, and the Others hot on their heels, the island survivors are constantly sprinting through the jungle for their very lives. It can be as physical as it appears, since all that speed is not from running in just one spot.

"There are a lot of ways we do that," explains Fong. "If there was a clearing, you could go handheld or steady cam but not for long. You can go sit on the back of those four-wheel vehicles that look like golf carts. You are hanging off the back with a handheld and they drive that thing and the person chases you. There is also the side view. Whenever you see a side view, chances are it is right next to some path or road."

"[For those Australian scenes with Kate] we couldn't get any cars that had steering wheels on the wrong side, so we shot everything and reversed the film."

Lost has so many outdoor sequences that lighting can be technical and tricky, especially at night around the burning fire. "Close ups are not lit by fire; it just looks that way," states Fong. "One thing we kept at was how to make it more natural. We worked on that and it evolved into a system that looked better during the series than the pilot. It started getting really easy but it is really cool because you have big spaces like the jungle or beach and no alleys. We don't have those special giant lights like in Hollywood so you learn about minimalism and how dark you can let it go while seeing what you need to see. That was a challenge and I think we pulled it off."

Fong remained with *Lost* throughout the first season but has since moved on to other projects such as Warner Brothers' recent big budgeted Persian/Spartan flick, *300*. Based on the Frank Miller graphic novel, the movie was also directed by one of Fong's friends, Zak Snyder. Immediately, he was struck by the differences between film and television. "You have a lot more time," offers Fong. "For *Lost*, you had eight days to shoot 46 minutes which is about seven pages a day. There is some second unit but it is like five or six pages a day in TV. For a movie, it is like three or four. You also don't use two cameras as much so you can really concentrate on a shot by shot scene. On TV, you have two cameras going all the time and if one is wide, it is like, 'Get the other camera. Just shoot the close up over there.' Sometimes there are compromises because of that. The way you want to work is one shot at a time so you can make every one perfect. On TV, there is just not time for that. That is an art too, knowing how to shoot multiple cameras. Another difference was the food [laughs]. Episode to episode, you have the same characters but the directors rotate. For a movie, you are working with the same director 60 days in a row. You can have a more cohesive vision and a longer form project.

"The coolest thing about television, other than being the most frantic form of cinema or film, is that you know it is going to be on air in a few weeks," he continues. "It has to be done and no matter what, it will be shown. It is not like when you do an indie and, 'Will it be shown for three days in an art house and then be thrown into a video bin?' The thing about *Lost*, love it or hate it, is over 20 million people will be watching it in a couple of weeks."

Reflecting on his time on *Lost*, Fong can't help but gush over the experience and how it has impacted his career. "It was totally rewarding," he concludes. "I've never done an episodic and had decided to take myself out of the commercial world because obviously when someone wants to be a film maker, they want to do long form and drama. I love commercials but they are 30-second stories and you really want something where people can sit down and say, 'That moved me, or I loved it, or I cried.' It would have been worth doing *Lost* for many reasons. Number one was to work with J.J., my good friend. Number two was to go to an amazing location. Number three is you always have to do projects that will make you grow. *Lost* was a way of letting people know I can do other things. Even though Zak wanted me to shoot *300*, without *Lost*, maybe people wouldn't have been so confident. Every project builds on the next." △

SCHOOL OF ROCK

BLACK ROCK
PORTSMOUTH

With exclusive photos from his own personal collection, Sculptor JIM VAN HOUTEN is about to blow the cover on one of the show's most intriguing discoveries, the eerie ship wreckage of the Black Rock…

"The set for the interior shots of the ship is about 40 miles away from the on-location wreckage – you go through the door in one place, and you come out the other side, miles and miles away – it's all movie magic [laughs]!"

GENESIS OF THE BLACK ROCK

It was originally going to only be a foreground miniature, but then the team decided it would be easier if the actors actually had a physical thing on location that they could actually walk up to. So I started by constructing a smaller version. Then we constructed the last 40-feet as life-size. It's built out of 24 styrofoam blocks which are 2' x 4' x 16' in size. From the smaller model I built, we constructed the full-size version, working from the outside in. In sculpture, you tend to work in a subtractive fashion. The kind of styrofoam we used is a new element in the motion picture film industry – maybe in the past 20 years. Before that they were mainly using plaster. With something like the inside of the hatch, a lot of the pipes are all made out of foam.

The full-size section of the Black Rock ended up being made up of four sections that were put on a giant truck that was taken to the shooting location. Then, a big piece of machinery set the pieces in place, and secured it, and then the team painted it. They did a great paint job – that's what really sold it. When you see the characters walk inside the ship, that's actually a set on a soundstage. So you can walk straight through the section of the Black Rock that was placed on location. The set for the interior shots of the ship is about 40 miles away from the on-location wreckage – you go through the door in one place, and you come out the other side, miles and miles away – it's all movie magic [laughs]!

THE ORIGINS OF THE SLAVE SHIP

I wasn't given a detailed back-story. Most of the direction given was, "It has to be an old wooden hulk of a ship," plus, "a long ship that was blown way inland on the island, perhaps from a tsunami or something." It had to be far enough away from the jungle and the beach so that when Hurley says, "How does something like that… get here?" it really has that feeling of, "Where did this come from?"

With this work, it's a little 'no guts no glory' – you have to take the ball and run. The timeframe that we have on the show is very small. A lot of the time you hope you're running down the right avenue with a certain idea. Sometimes you're wrong, but generally you get a feel for it.

All of the ideas come from the writers, and they're verbal, so they describe what they're seeing with words, but of course, you can't peak into their minds [laughs], so by working with the art department and asking as many questions as you can – but you know, with time, sometimes you just have to be all, "go go go!"

RETURNING TO THE BLACK ROCK'S MYSTERY

I don't know if we're going back there or not… maybe. I hope we get to go back to that Black Rock, but for the moment, it sure doesn't look that way. The thing is, film and television are such visual art forms, we're telling our stories through these pictures, and a lot of the time, something that we're seemingly working weeks on, you'll only get a glimpse of, and that's it! But that does add to the mystery of the story as well: you see it, you leave and then it's, "What was that?" But I do think that sometimes it's more fun for the audience to fill in the blanks.

A lot of cinema right now, you can figure out what the movie's about during the opening credits [laughs]! I like films that, for the first 45 minutes or so you're like, "What the heck am I watching?" – you don't know what's going on but can't take your eyes off the screen. ☠

LOST

201

Thanks to the *Lost* Production Office, here are the original designs for the infamous tunnel that led Kate, Locke and Jack to Desmond, and the frustrating countdown conundrum...

4 8 15
23 16
42

MIRROR
A

108

TUNNEL VISION

201

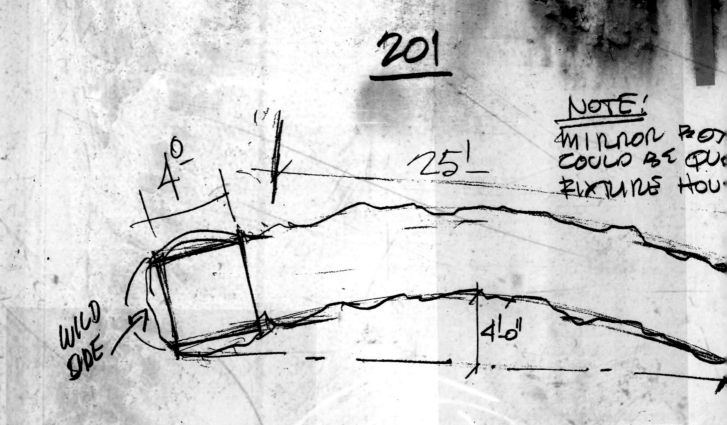

NOTE:
MIRROR BOT
COULD BE QU
FIXTURE HOU

1'
4'0"
25'
4'0"
WILD SIDE

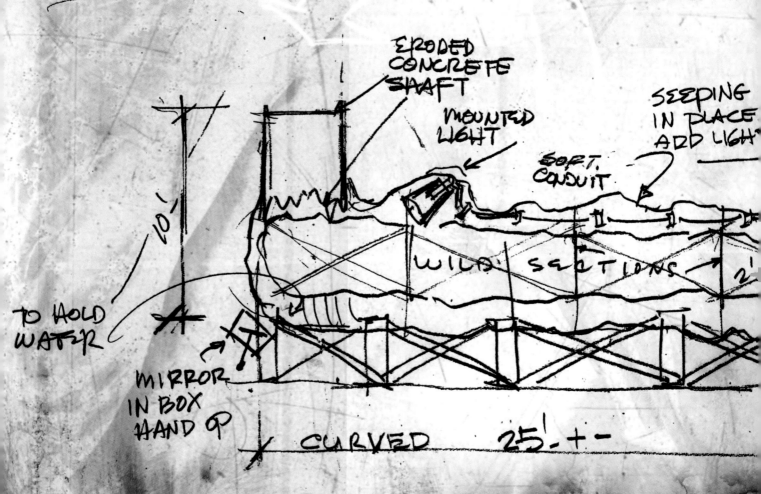

ERODED
CONCRETE
SHAFT

MOUNTED
LIGHT

SEEPING
IN PLACE
ADD LIGH

SOFT.
CONDUIT

WILD SECTIONS

10'

2'

TO HOLD
WATER

MIRROR
IN BOX
HAND OP

CURVED   25' +-

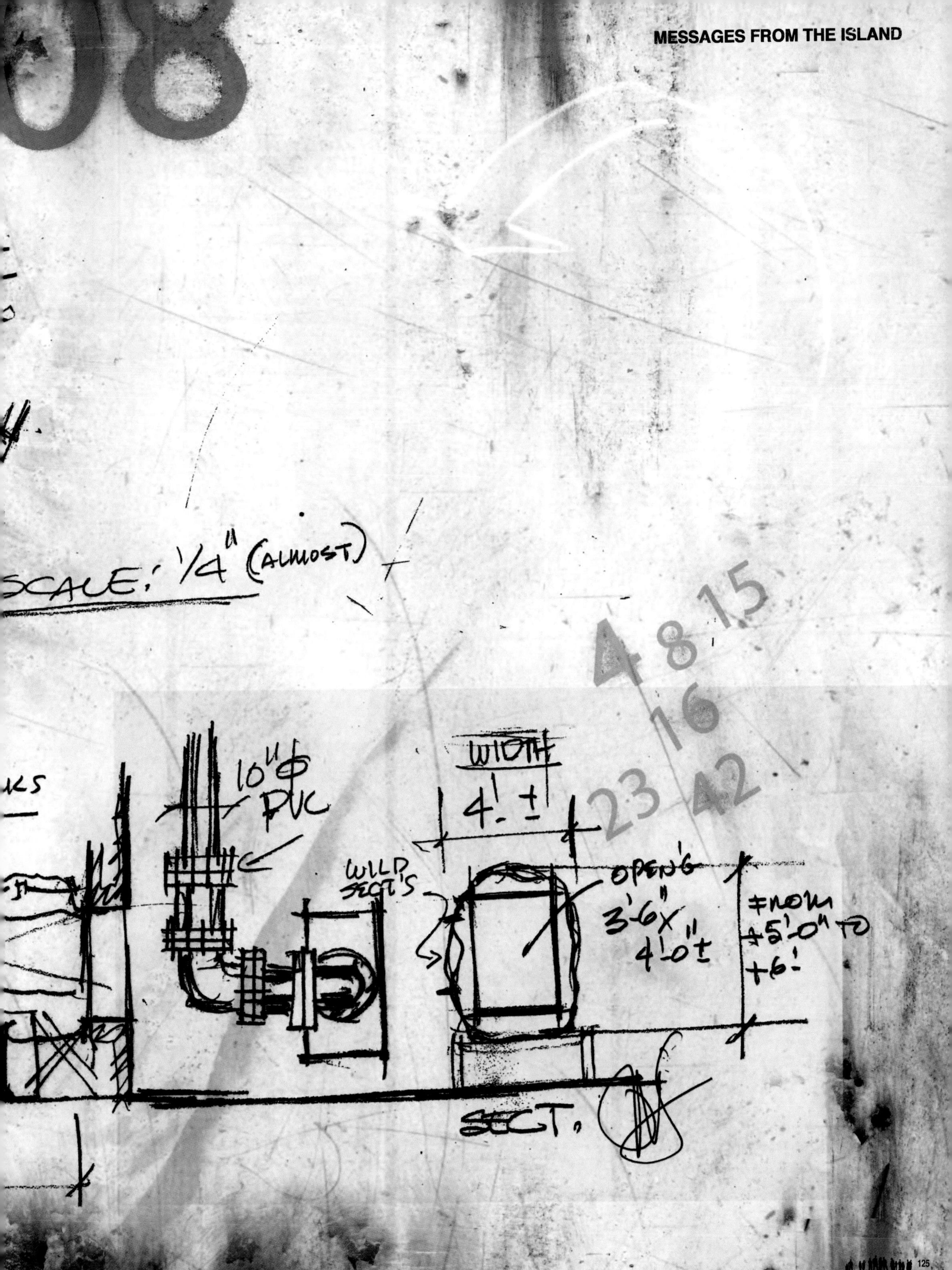
08
SCALE: 1/4" (ALMOST)
4 8 15
16
23 42
WIDTH
4'-±
10"Φ
PVC
WILD SECT'S
OPEN'G
3'-6" X
4'-0"±
FROM
+5'-0" TO
+6'
SECT.

THREE SIDES TO EVERY STORY

MATTHEW FOX, EVANGELINE LILLY, and JOSH HOLLOWAY talk about their characters' tangled web of truth, lies, lust and love…

None will ever argue that *Lost* isn't an ensemble show, but that certainly doesn't negate the fact that over two seasons, an absorbing romantic triangle has unfolded which has equally engaged and frustrated loyal viewers. Cleverly representing the vast differences in the personalities marooned on the island, Jack Shephard (Matthew Fox), Kate Austen (Evangeline Lilly) and James 'Sawyer' Ford (Josh Holloway) have elicited extreme passion, anger, and pain from one another. Trying to find their place among the wreckage of their lives, both literally and figuratively, these three people have pushed one another to expose their true natures, and perhaps their ultimate destinies.

In the case of Jack and Sawyer, it's always been about position and respect. Sawyer despises the trust that the survivors have for the good doctor and so he's made it his goal to be a constant thorn in Jack's side. In turn, Jack hates Sawyer's selfish goals and his predatory hoarding of vital supplies that puts lives in jeopardy. Yet for Sawyer and Kate, it's all about their link as kindred spirits with wicked pasts. Together they make combustible chemistry, but they also share a secret empathy for each other's pain and unwise life decisions.

Meanwhile, the other side of the triangle connects Kate and Jack, who bonded from the moment they met on the island beach. Since then, they share an undeniable attraction for one another and yet, their natures also push them apart, with Kate feeling unworthy of Jack's attentions and Jack being hurt and disillusioned by her deeply checkered past.

Over two seasons, their stories have become absolutely interwoven and it's a connection that the actors happily embrace. Now, *Lost Magazine* talks exclusively to all three of the actors about the growth of their characters, the challenges of the last season, and who they really think will finally capture Kate's heart once and for all…

> "If it weren't for the Others and the Tailies, it would have been easy for all our characters to just maintain the status quo. That's probably been the strength of season two, it has really mixed it up and kept it alive." – Evangeline Lilly

The dynamic of *Lost* really changed immediately at the start of season two. The core cast was fractured apart and there were new cast members added. Was that, to a degree, disconcerting?
Matthew Fox: No, I thought it was going to be really exciting and I think it has been. I really loved the idea of the Tailies coming into the show and what that would mean to the whole dynamic of *Lost*. I was very excited about that and think it's been a really interesting year and has worked out well.
Evangeline Lilly: I think the addition of the Tailies was brilliant. I know that it was an awkward transition for the audience – I know that there were a lot of people who were excited about it and a lot of people that were uncomfortable about it – but I think in the end, it kept the island alive. It would have been very easy for the island to become stale. There is only so long that people are going to sit on a deserted island with the same united group before it becomes completely static. The new struggles that we encountered through the turmoil of different people being thrown together was unexpected. If it weren't for the Others and the Tailies, it would have been easy for all our characters to just maintain the status quo. That's probably been the strength of season two, it has really mixed it up and kept it alive.
Josh Holloway: I loved that! I was really excited about getting to do that – when we split and did the raft thing. I was glad I was a part of that, even though it was some of the hardest work we've ever done because it was all on the water! So coming back for the second season, we knew damn well that we were starting right where we left off: we were right back in the water. We started off the season with such a bang – I came cursing out of the water, screaming, and it's at night and there

NOVEL IDEA

JOSH HOLLOWAY & EVANGELINE LILLY
discuss which books they think best represent their characters…

JH: I'm a reader and I love reading. I think a good book would be Ayn Rand's *Atlas Shrugged*. I read *Robinson Crusoe* when we were doing the pilot, which I thought was good too. *Watership Down* is a great book and animated film as well. It's a great story that has all the implications of *Lord of the Flies* in the rabbit world.
EL: I think Ayn Rand's *Atlas Shrugged* is a great book too – I was actually given that book by Josh [laughs]! It doesn't necessarily precisely depict Kate but could represent her in a strong way. He gave it to me for my birthday in season one, August 3rd. I didn't read it until mid-way through season two, but I have been perpetually reminding him of it because it made such an impact on me. Josh and I have both chuckled many times over the fact that Sawyer and Kate are so similar to Josh and I. We have very tight correlations to our characters, so for us to both love that book and swear by that book… it doesn't surprise me that we say that our characters could easily be represented by it.

was lots of swimming [to do], and the bullet [wound]! So it was really an intense beginning, which I love. I love to be thrown right into the fire.

I also love working with Harold [Perrineau] and Daniel [Dae Kim]. It was really cool because it tightened our relationships as characters and also as people, which was great because I hadn't gotten to do a lot of scenes with them [beforehand], except when we started on the raft. I love that it formed a bond between those three characters and it added a new dynamic to the relationships on the island.

And then of course, immediately, we meet the other people. I've been a fan of Adewale's [Mr. Eko] for a while. I followed him on *Oz*, loved him in that, and I couldn't wait to meet the guy. And the first time I met him… he smacks me in the face with a stick – that's our introduction [laughs]! Great! So that was fun and we went right into that tiger trap. That was interesting because we actually did it in a hole. They dug a hole and it was hilarious because you have three actors, a cameraman, the focus puller *and* the sound guy – they plopped us all in there! And it was like a pig farm because it's kind of stinky and that mud is full of all kinds of stuff [laughs]!

> *"Who knows, one of us could get infected or maybe we become Others, like in The Thing when it gets in your body and you don't know which one has it."*
> *– Josh Holloway*

SUMMER HOLIDAY

MATTHEW FOX, **EVANGELINE LILLY** & **JOSH HOLLOWAY**
talk about their plans for the summer hiatus…

Josh, your character was injured in the first third of the season, so there was a forced vulnerability that we got to see from Sawyer. Were you comfortable playing him in that position?

JH: I loved it and was challenged by it the whole time. The hardest part was the physicality of it because I had to slowly deteriorate and then pass out. I'd never done that as an actor. I remember pulling Harold aside going, "Dude, I've never passed out! Do you have any hints of what *not* to do?" He said, "You are good, just go for it." As far as the vulnerability, I liked that and thought it was good for the character. I loved trying to keep his bravado – even when he is going down, he is still being a smart ass [laughs]!

There have been some great episodes that revealed some darker backgrounds to each of your characters. Starting with Jack, more of his history was revealed in the episodes *Man of Science, Man of Faith* and *The Hunting Party*. Matthew, were you surprised by any of the new details you were provided about your character?

MF: I'm always surprised to learn the things that Damon Lindelof has got in his mind about what's happened to Jack Shephard in his past. This year in [*The Hunting Party*] we find out what happened to his marriage. It was a tough episode and I really enjoyed doing it. I was surprised, but at the same time, with my conversations with Damon, I had some inkling how that relationship was going to come to an end and how that would define who Jack Shephard is. That episode also really left us with [a sense of], "What is going to be next for him?" I'm very much looking forward to seeing what happens to him *after* that marriage has come to an end. I have a feeling it's going to be pretty dark and a painful period in Jack Shephard's life. It may be the back-story where we find out what all the tattoo art means to him. I am looking forward to it. I always do. I look forward to every script on *Lost* with great anticipation.

Matthew Fox is starring in the movie *We Are… Marshall*, which began shooting at the tail end of season two…

MF: For me, it's always about the story and *We Are… Marshall* is based on actual events. The real story is incredibly powerful and is an example of the strength of the human spirit. Then you put that into a script form and bring together all the people who have been brought together… it's such a great cast and McG is directing it. Everybody is so incredibly passionate about it and it just had all the elements that I am always looking for – a wonderful story that has the potential to be very powerful in a movie, and then a lot of people that really believe in it and care about it. It's been great so far, and I have six more weeks of it when we finish season two."

JH: Honestly? I don't want to work, but if a project came up that I loved, I would be compelled to go. I would love to take a hiatus off and go to Europe with my wife. We loved our RV trip so much in Alaska last year; we are going to do a little one – get an RV in LA and just take off. I don't know where we will go. I want a vacation, but if Oliver Stone or the Coen Brothers suddenly want to work with me…I'm there [laughs]!

EL: I'm actually in a position where I feel like I want to enjoy my time off. I don't want to work. We work really hard through the year and we earn some time off. Now that I've gotten comfortable [with the 'celebrity' aspect] and I'm not squirming anymore, I want to sit back and enjoy it for at least one hiatus. Last hiatus was hectic! I did press, work, and my head was spinning, and I traveled, too. This hiatus I want to sit back and enjoy where I've come from and what's become of my career and life and reap some of the benefits of that. In the hiatus of 2007, I will approach and tackle the world of film. By that time, I think that I will have rested long enough to be at a comfortable place in television, so then I will be up for the challenge.

"I've been a fan of Adewale's [Mr. Eko] for a while. I followed him on Oz, loved him in that, and I couldn't wait to meet the guy. And the first time I met him... he smacks me in the face with a stick – that's our introduction [laughs]!"

– Josh Holloway

Was Sawyer's dark turn in *The Long Con* hard to swallow or a welcome return to form in your eyes, Josh?

JH: That episode was a blast and a shock to me when I first got it. I had been playing this vulnerable guy that was finally getting along [with everyone]. When I got that script and I read it, I was like, "Oh my! What would make him do that?" and that is what you have to find as an actor. It was simply because he had to take his power back. In his own mind, he was becoming impotent with conforming to the group. He was like, "Wait a second. I don't want any part of this." Plus, he had lost most of his stash. They took most of his stuff so he didn't have any more power to control the things he wanted. So he figured, "I'm going to take my teeth back [laughs]!" But it took me a minute to adjust inside because in my own mind, I wouldn't do that. After that, I would continue to, hopefully, grow, but in Sawyer's mind, doing that *is* growing and getting back on top. He's an alpha male, and that's his way of doing it. I think a lot of it is not about hoarding the guns. It was simply to show people, "Watch your back. I'm not kidding around."

Evangeline, when we finally found out *What Kate Did*, did that revelation adjust your own expectations of her history?

EL: I think a real testament to the strength and integrity of our writers is that, that script – as far as how little it surprised me, I feel like I could have closed my eyes and written it in my sleep. How the writers had already portrayed Kate: where they had brought her from, where they were taking her to, what was happening in her heart and mind, and who she was as a human being, they were so on the money with all of those surrounding details and factors. They were totally congruent and I felt what she had done and how she had dealt with it all made sense. It worked for where she is now as a result of those events. On the island, reading that Kate was basically going out of her mind was such a relief to me – so many times in this show things have gone wrong on the island and I have felt that if I was Kate, I would have a complete breakdown. I would lose control and wouldn't be able to handle it – I would be a blubbering mess. To be able to do that, it was like this tension and energy that you put into every episode finally got to explode [laughs]. Again, I feel like since then there is another Kate: she is different again in a completely new way from the rest of the season.

Did the appearance of the horse in the episode have a specific representation in your mind?

EL: I don't know the *actual* symbolism of the horse, but I did feel that the role the horse played in the flashback, combined with the role the horse played on the island, was very symbolic. Not only was it a turning point in both stories, but it was also a bit of a supernatural foundation in both those stories. When Kate is able to reach out and touch that horse at the end of the episode, it's where her salvation comes from. It's what brings her from being insane, unstable and potentially going over the edge, to her feeling in some way, shape or form, that she touched God, or her soul, or something untouchable, that has proved her sanity. There is a grace for her. I might be reading too much into it, but I really feel that is what happened – a grace was passed through that connection. When she has that moment with Jack, right before the kiss where she says to him, "I just can't... I can't... I can't." She doesn't specify what she can or can't do, except for, "I can't." I feel like maybe after that moment with the horse, it's like she is given the grace so that she can believe in herself. In the whole episode, she thinks she has seen a ghost, but then the ghost turns out to be real and I think it sends her a message to believe in herself.

A TIME TO HEAL

JOSH HOLLOWAY discusses the challenges of recovering from his bullet wound...

"The only problem I had was when I talked to the director and said, 'I've been shot in the shoulder, dude. How long is this going to take to heal, because I want to play more of the reality of it, but we are on a TV show?' And they were like, 'Yeah, you are wounded and we are going to play it, but the TV gods are smiling too, so you'll be healing quick.' So the whole time after that was a challenge. They put me right away running off with Jack and Locke in the jungle two or three days after I got back. I was like, '*OK*?' I tried to play it as much as they would allow. Also, the island does have these healing properties, which they've touched on more and more – it keeps coming up. It's part of the island's mystery, and I was like, 'OK, they convinced me *that* way.'"

Jack has been a perfect study in what happens when a resolute fixer can't make anything actually work the way he wants. Matthew, has your character's inability to control anything in his life on this island been frustrating for you as well?

MF: Absolutely. There is no question, but I do think that is his lot in these circumstances. This idea of needing to control, fix, repair and tackle problems with the zeal and intensity that he does, I think it's a very male thing. Most men would tell you that, in their relationships with women in their lives, one of the things they get accused of often is attempting to fix things too much. I think you can really generalize the difference between the genders when it comes to when a woman is upset about something, it's very difficult for the male gender to just be there. It translates almost immediately for most men for a need to make it go away. This defining part of Jack Shephard is connected to 'control' – he has an intense need to control the circumstances in which he exists and to fix the problems that come into that.

I think that is a really common part of all of human nature. It does become very frustrating when you are dealing with the circumstances that Jack Shephard is dealing with and the complexities of the island, and the many things and types of people he can't control or fix. Sometimes, I, because I am playing him, feel completely powerless. But that is what *he* would feel, that a lot of the time – almost always – he is not accomplishing what he wants to get done. If you look back through the year and look at the amount of things he has tackled and what he has accomplished in fixing – it's not very many [laughs]! It's frustrating, but its just part of what the character is existing in.

LOST

Do you guys ever get frustrated about Sawyer and Kate's characterization/journey?

JH: You don't want to limit what your character can do. That's what's hard. Once they have a life like this, and you care about them, you do get your own ideas: "I think Sawyer should be doing this or he should be doing that," and you really feel justified in saying it somehow. It's hilarious, but you can't do that as an actor, because you then limit what your character can do – you've already thrown a judgment on where you can go. I was thinking I would like for my guy to be nicer and when I got that [script for *The Long Con*], I was like, "Why does he have to be mean again?" But I *got* it.

EL: I like to leave the mysteries of the show, the character and the arcs in the hands of the producers and the writers. I feel a great deal of respect for the people who created and maintain this show. I also feel that there is a real foundation in the structure of how things are maintained on the show. I don't like to disrupt that structure, so I tend to leave all that to the producers. It doesn't mean that, quietly, in my own mind, I don't hope for things, but I never voice them to the powers that be. That is, unless somewhere along the line something has gone unnoticed, or something has slipped under their noses and there is a breach in character.

As far as anticipating what Kate is going to do or where she is going to go, I leave it up to them. It turns out that she really did change from the beginning of season two to the end of season two in a completely opposite way than I anticipated. I wanted her to grow in her independence on the island and not trail around after the men on the island, helping them in their endeavors. In that, I thought there would be a real hardening, that Kate would go back to the darker side that we saw in her in the beginning of season one. What ended up happening was the complete opposite. If anything, she became softer and more vulnerable and more caring and giving. She hasn't spent most of the season trailing around after Jack or with Sawyer, but she has been, for the most part of the season, at the bedside of the sick and holding the hands of the weary and allowing people to cry on her shoulder. I think she has become the heart of the island in some way. I don't know if that is because she is healed, or because she feels so confused or tormented that it's easier for her to care for others than herself.

When the original cast reunited by mid-season, how was it meshing again with your fellow peers?

EL: For the season one regular characters, when we made that return back to the old formula, I think every single one of us, when we would meet on the set, we would meet eyes and breathe a sigh of relief. For us it was like we were home. It was so nice to get back to a place that we knew and we understood and believed in because we were treading in really unfamiliar waters in the first quarter of this season. For some of us, we couldn't grasp where we fit in that new mold. Basically, it was like starting from scratch again. Even as audience members, we all felt that if we were just watching the show, we would be craving the formula because it had grown into the story we knew and loved of *Lost*.

JH: Yeah, we were eager to work with each other, but it was odd at first. There were big hugs with, "Aw, *finally*! Hey, stranger!" and those kinds of things. We still saw each other off set, but it was good, like coming home. It had a good familiar feeling, but at the same time, we had made all these new relationships. It was like an adventure and then coming back to the good feeling of family, and now we have more family members.

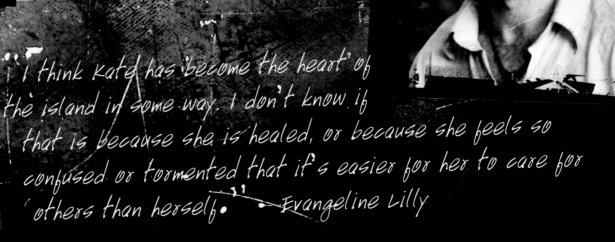

"I think Kate has become the heart of the island in some way. I don't know if that is because she is healed, or because she feels so confused or tormented that it's easier for her to care for others than herself." — Evangeline Lilly

This season, Kate seems to have a better clarity of herself and even how she looks at Jack and Sawyer too...

EL: I totally agree, because I feel like she is almost able to see everything from a more separated place. She doesn't have to be emotionally involved because I think a lot of what held her to those men was her need to feel worthy in some way. A lot of the time she would chase Jack and help because she didn't know how else to be useful. She didn't have any other way of feeling worthy and I think what's happening is she is seeing she isn't the only flawed person on this island. Jack has flaws and makes mistakes. Sawyer has some serious flaws but she can see strength in his core. She is realizing she is an equal with many. Before she had a real inferiority problem, and now she can look at them and chuckle, because she sees they need to get over themselves. She is digging those guys in the ribs more about the whole triangle.

With the shift in how Kate sees herself, do you look at the romantic triangle differently and who you think she should gravitate towards more?

EL: I definitely do see a shift there. I feel that, as Kate is moving into season three, both of those men are going to have to chase her because she is going to be a bit blind to them. She is now in a place where she is done chasing them – both of them. If either of them wants her attention or respect, they are going to have to give a little and put their best foot forward or at least a foot forward. Up to now, Jack has never put in an ounce of effort with Kate. He's become attracted and repelled, but he hasn't actually put in any effort for her. Sawyer has, but the only effort he has put out is to get her in the sack. He's never put an ounce of emotional effort into her. I think she is at a place where she sees through them both and she is done with it. I think she has reached out to both of them in a really vulnerable way and has been hurt.

With the kiss between Jack and Kate and their strengthening bond into the finale, do you see Jack as more of a real match for her?

MF: Yeah, I think that these two people have reached a point where they are more accepting of who the other person is. When that happens, then there is a really deep attraction, not just physically, but emotionally – a need. I think that's what stood in the way of these two people for a long time. It's certainly what stood in the way of Jack as far as his need and desire, emotionally, to her. He wasn't as accepting of her flaws. I think the circumstances of the island are becoming more and more intense and getting to be more accepting of each other's shortcomings leaves that desire, which has always been there and if anything has only been growing, for an emotional connection, and leaves it more open for that to happen. In the two years that we have been doing this show, and the couple of months that these two people have existed in these circumstances on the island – right now is the closest they have ever been. When you see how the year ends, it's going to be really interesting to see where it goes next year.

So Josh, where does that leave Sawyer in the mix?

JH: I am so interested to see where that goes, but regardless, either [Jack] or Sawyer better get some action – it's ridiculous [laughs]! But seriously, these characters are really alive now. Sawyer will always screw it up, because he's Sawyer. He is all caught up in it now and he's got feelings for her and there is nothing he can do about it. She's got him in a way. If the audience expects it, you better believe it ain't gonna happen. These writers throw twists all the time, so that's cool. If the fans expect it, I can pretty much determine that I ain't gonna get her [laughs].

"Sometimes, I, because I am playing Jack, feel completely powerless. But that is what he would feel, that a lot of the time – almost always – he is not accomplishing what he wants to get done." – Matthew Fox

In the last half of the season, the character alignments and relationships have really shifted in surprising directions. Where do you anticipate it heading for the next season?

MF: One of the things that I anticipated this year was that it has got more *Lord of the Flies*-ish. Amongst our core group of people, these betrayals and alliances began to ebb and flow and get complicated. I always anticipated that something bigger than that core was going to challenge them – that being the Others. What you have is a situation where these characters in our core group have really intense dynamics amongst themselves, whether they have alliances or whether they are really at odds with one another, like Jack and Sawyer. Suddenly, you are thrown into a situation where there is another line drawn with another group.

JH: I think [the tensions] will continue forever. I keep saying 'Alpha Men,' but the thing is, none of them are followers, so there is always going to be a power struggle. They all have their attributes, though I don't really know what Sawyer's is yet [laughs]! Jack is a doctor, Sayid is a soldier, Locke is a philosopher, Sawyer is... the axe in the wheel? I don't know where that will go, but it will twist and turn. There will be alliances within the camp, and I don't think the camp will split up yet. I see that happening as the show continues in a few years. Who knows, one of us could get infected or maybe we become Others – like in *The Thing* when it gets in your body and you don't know which one has it. I can see them go off into so many directions, but I have no fricken clue. I love it now because before I was trying to think ahead. Now, I am just enjoying Hawaii and loving work. I get a script and go do it because I know it will be kick-ass.

> "I would like to see more of these new alliances. For example, Charlie and Mr. Eko who knows where that is going to lead in season three..."
> – Evangeline Lilly

EL: What I would like to see, as an audience member, is more of these new alliances. For example, Charlie spent the whole first season wooing Claire and spent most of the second season in No Man's Land – but we now see an alliance with him and Mr. Eko – who knows where that is going to lead in season three...

For Kate, she spent a lot of the first season primarily with the men on the island and in season two, you see her interacting with a lot of the women on the island. With all of these new shifts and alliances, I would like to see another side to the characters so they become more full.

We didn't get to see Jack or Locke tempered the way we see them when they are put together, and that is so true of humanity and how we interact with other human beings. You might be the most congenial person in the world for 10 years running with the same person, but you spend 10 minutes with a different person who brings out another side of you... you might be a total monster with them. I love that aspect, but it also scares me because it's a lot of people to keep straight. One of my concerns for the show and the characters is the difficulty of the thru-line. What worries me is that there isn't time or room to explore those sides and they will be left hanging. The audience will only get a glimpse or taste of it and then all they will see after that is the same old thing. To really have these characters live, they have to maintain that after they have introduced it. It's a huge challenge.

STAR-CROSSED LOVERS?

MATTHEW FOX explains where he feels Jack and Kate are at right now…

"They are now emotionally connected more intensely than they have ever been. If you removed all the circumstances that are getting in the way of them being together romantically, I think they could be together at this point. But there are so many things going on and so many things requiring their attention and their energy, it's like two ships constantly passing in the night, but they really are connected through time and space almost."

" *I'm very much looking forward to seeing what happens [in Jack's flashbacks] after that marriage has come to an end. I have a feeling it's going to be pretty dark and a painful period in Jack Shephard's life.*" – Matthew Fox

How do you feel going into the third season of the series?

JH: I like where [Sawyer's] position is now. It's fun. I'm hoping there is some kind of clash with the Others.

EL: I actually just feel really eager. I was very hesitant and apprehensive about going from season one to season two, because I was afraid to keep going at this job. I was so nervous. Now, coming out of season two it couldn't be more opposite. I am eager to see where they take the show in season three because they have done this really incredible thing of making each season a chapter in and of itself.

There is a distinct life to season one that is totally different from season two. I can't wait to see what the 'character' of season three is! I have now also gotten to a place of comfort with Kate and that brings me to another level. I might get a little bit more involved with making suggestions for my character in season three. I have not done that yet, but I know, being a writer myself, that sometimes the inkwell runs dry and you want input. It can be very helpful for the characters to bring some new ideas to the table. Now that I feel that I am finally at a place where I understand Kate and understand what the writers are doing with her, maybe I can get involved with where Kate goes and who she becomes. It's exciting!

MF: You put Jack and Sawyer in really, really dire circumstances – which is where they will be next year – and with Kate in the mix of that triangle, then you watch people have to deal with something larger than themselves. Watching those relationships come together, even with everything that is between them, is very interesting, and in my mind that is what season three is going to be about. ◊

"*Everyone is staring at the ocean behind me with their jaws dropped to the ground...*"

"I think the moment when I was most in awe of my 'office,' as I call it, was when my parents were in town visiting. I was doing a scene where I started out with my back to the ocean and I was supposed to walk up the beach towards Jack. I'm waiting for the call for, 'Action,' and it's not coming... and it's not coming... and it's not coming. Finally, I look around and I'm like, 'Helloooo? When are we going to go?' Everyone around me, crew, cast, everyone, is staring at the ocean behind me with their jaws dropped to the ground and their eyes bugging out of their heads. I turn around, and maybe 20 to 50 feet from the shore, so close to us, was this massive, beautiful mother Grey whale that was jumping out of the water; I believe they call it 'breeching.' She was teaching her little baby whale how to do this, so they were breeching and jumping together and leaping out of the water, and it went on and on and on. We actually stopped filming and just watched this majestic display of nature for half and hour and then finally we had to get back to work. It was incredible, and it was amazing that my parents were there to experience it."

Think you've seen every inch of The Swan?
Think again as we take you deeper into the
hatch than you've ever been before...

Super-computer or elaborate ruse? It's The Swan's attention-demanding centerpiece...

Not a bad couch considering most of the furniture is from the 1970s...

The home gymnasium doubles up as Jack's E.R. (complete with blood-soaked bandages and a rather dubious looking operating table/towel)...

At least while you're on Hatch duty you get to rest in a proper bed, as opposed to roughing it on the beach

It's The Swan bathroom sink – complete with a classy bathmat that looks like a concrete vent...

It wouldn't be 'Locke's Hatch' without a game of backgammon in mid-flow...

The kitchen area is pretty well equipped, although we haven't seen too many cups of tea or coffee made...

Another intricate
part of The Swan's
mechanical underbelly

It's the room that has
been equally a blessing
and a curse – the
Dharma pantry...

DI 9FFTR731

BEETS

DI 9FFTR731

COOKIES

COOKIES

What do you think all of these dials mean? Our crash survivors haven't got a clue...

What every Hatch employee needs – a twin-speed Dharma washing machine complete with dryer...

DI 9FFTR731

DHARMA INITIATIVE MACARONI & CHEESE SUPPER

On this bottom row of exclusive pictures, we present to you a selection of Dharma's finest products, from beets to shaving balm...

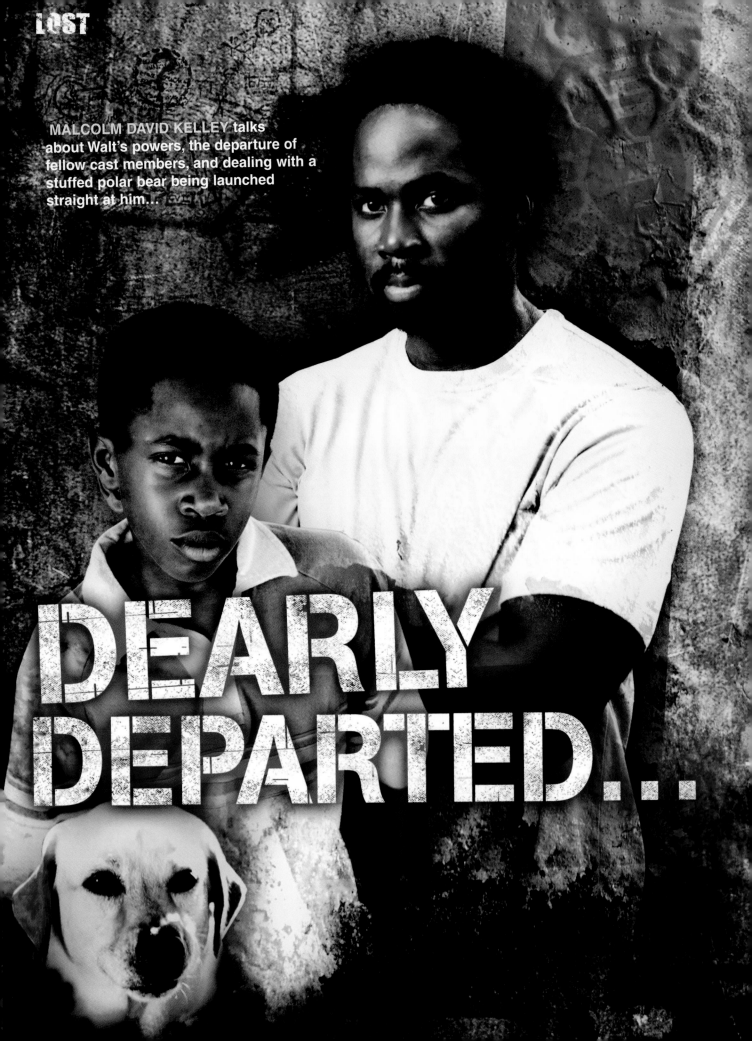

MALCOLM DAVID KELLEY talks about Walt's powers, the departure of fellow cast members, and dealing with a stuffed polar bear being launched straight at him…

DEARLY DEPARTED…

"One of the things they did with the polar bear was a greenscreen. Then they had a head and some arms flying at me, which really didn't help at all because I was laughing all the time [laughs]!"

How did you find the audition experience for *Lost*?
It was a regular audition. J.J. Abrams and Damon Lindelof were there and I just went in not expecting anything. I went in, did my best, hoped for the best, got a callback, and the next thing you know they are telling me I'm going to Hawaii [smiles]!

Did you get together with Harold Perrineau to establish the father/son dynamic?
I was the last one to come to Hawaii. Everybody was already cast and over there having a good time. But as soon as I got there, Harold and I bonded really quickly. He was like my family out there because I didn't really know anyone in Hawaii. I got to know everybody, but Harold and I got very close. I was at his house almost every day playing video games, watching TV, and hanging out.

Do you think Michael was a good father?
From the show, people have doubts about him now and whether he's gone bad because he shot Ana Lucia and Libby. But he was trying to get his son back.

Strange things happen around Walt. Do you think he has psychic or supernatural abilities?
Yeah, he has powers, but just doesn't know it yet. At the end, he has a tendency to make things happen which is cool. Walt doesn't know how to use them or that they exist but as soon as he finds out, I think he's going to put those powers to good use.

It did seem that perhaps Walt brought the polar bear to life out of the comic book... what memories do you have of the sequence where it attacks you?
It was hard because first of all, one of the things they did with the polar bear was a greenscreen. Then they had a head and some arms flying at me, which really didn't help at all because I was laughing all the time [laughs]! I had to dig deep down and use my acting skills to start crying. I liked the way it turned out.

Walt loves comic books. Do you share that passion?
I'm into video games but not so much comic books. I'm more into the sports games like basketball, football, and soccer. I love the graphics.

At one point, Walt and Locke were spending time together. What made the two good friends?
Locke was somebody Walt could talk to. He didn't treat Walt like a kid. Locke would teach him how to do things and they would hang out. It was like having a best friend, but then my Dad cut that relationship short so I didn't get to talk to him anymore.

Harold has a fear when it comes to water, but did you enjoy being on the raft with Sawyer, Michael and Jin last season?
It was cool but I was a little nervous that I might have to get in the water with the sharks and all the stuff in Hawaii. If I had to, I would have done it but luckily I didn't have to. Before that, I was swimming with Harold off set to make sure he could. He knows how to swim but not really well yet. He's working on it though. He can paddle.

What did you think of Walt being kidnapped by the Others?
I thought it was really good. Just the storyline itself – nobody expected that to happen. It was an exciting season finale.

Were you sad about not being in season two as much?
Yes, but during the first season I wanted to come home, but in the second season, I wanted to go back to Hawaii because I wasn't there as much [smiles]. I liked the second season better because it gave me the opportunity to work on different things like *My Name is Earl* and *Law & Order: Special Victims Unit*. All of that was fun – being home with my friends – before going back to Hawaii. Every time I go to Hawaii, it's like a vacation. It is beautiful out there.

Why do you think Walt appeared to Shannon out in the jungle?
He was trying to tell her something but kind of did it at the wrong time.

Did you know Shannon was going to be killed by Ana? Do they give you the whole script or only select pages?
Sometimes they try and keep it from the people who aren't shooting it, but word does get around on set. Otherwise, we don't know until they tell us in the moment. The next thing you know you are filming it!

So are you shocked when characters like Boone, Shannon, Libby, and Ana Lucia get bumped off?
Yeah, and it is sad to see them go like that because we all bonded really quickly. We had our own little family and then all of a sudden, they leave. We miss them, but they come back to visit, and we see them at events sometimes. We miss them a lot.

Which do you prefer filming – the island scenes or the flashbacks?
Probably the island stuff – just being on the beach and the caves. The flashbacks are still in Hawaii and it's like five minutes away from the set. You can still go over for lunch.

What was your opinion of this year's finale?
I thought last year's had a lot more suspense, but this one was pretty good. You can't argue with it. It was great and I love the show.

If Walt does come back, what would you want them to explore with your character?
His background a little bit more. We covered a lot in the flashbacks but there is more to him that we don't know about.

Do you have a memorable experience while working in Hawaii?
I've been snorkeling four times in one of the big spots. I also met some friends out there, so that has been fun. I go to school there, relax, and play basketball. I've played basketball with Harold and his wife because she used to play in college.

Are you working over the summer?
I just finished up this charity event last Saturday. It was amazing. It was a workshop we are sponsoring and the charity I'm with right now is called First Star. Otherwise, it has been a lot of interviews, auditions, and traveling a bit.

Has the success of *Lost* changed your life? Are you getting recognized on the street?
I get recognized a little bit more. When I did *Antwone Fisher* and *You Got Served*, that was more with the younger crowd, and *Lost* is more with the adults. It's pretty cool and I'm getting scripts now and no one ever sent me scripts before. 🔥

THE BIRTH OF

There are so many elements that come together to make *Lost* the unique viewing experience that it is week after week. The tremendous performances, gorgeous cinematography and inspired direction are just a few pieces among the myriad components that snap together to create each episode. Yet everyone agrees – from the producers, to the production team, and all the way to the audience – that the scripts are truly where the magic of *Lost* originates. Led by Executive Producers Damon Lindelof and Carlton Cuse, the *Lost* writing team toil together in a conference room on the Disney lot in Burbank, California, thrashing out ideas and "breaking" (short for breaking down) the stories that will be the focus of the 24 individual episodes that make up an entire season. While the team works together to determine the important beats for each episode, and where they will all land in the five-act structure used for each epiosde, there are individual writers who must then take that outline away and breathe life into the story.

During season two, *Lost* Writers' Assistants Dawn Lambertsen-Kelly and Matt Ragghianti were given the opportunity of their careers when they got the chance to pen their first script for broadcast television – the Claire-centric *Maternity Leave*. Over the course of a hectic, terrifying and absolutely thrilling four months, Kelly and Ragghianti gave *Lost Magazine* exclusive, behind-the-scenes access as they prepared, wrote and finally watched their creative baby evolve from script-to-screen. Through interviews, personal emails and photos, the writers share the realities of being first-time television writers, ultimately making some *Lost* magic of their own…

GETTING THE ASSIGNMENT

Both Kelly and Ragghianti were feature film scriptwriters before they landed gigs as writers' assistants on *Lost* during the early days of the series. They spent their first year on the show learning the dynamics of the Writers' Room and the intricacies of each script by alternating as the assistant in the room for the breaking of every episode. Each would take meticulous notes on the discussions and story points developed for each story by the writing team, keeping track of all details that would eventually make up the outline for each episode. Then the notes would be transferred to add to the ever-evolving show reference bible. Paying their dues and soaking up as much they could about the writing process throughout season one, Damon Lindelof rewarded them with the news they most wanted to hear – that they would be paired to write their own episode.

It was the opportunity the duo had been hoping for, and Matt Ragghianti remembers, "They told us at the end of season [one]. There are two freelance episodes per year [on one-hour dramas] that are required by the Writers' Guild. One had already been assigned to Drew Goddard (*Outlaws*) and then the second one was coming up. We were hopeful that we would be assigned that one and then in fact it went to a woman named Janet Tamaro, who did a wonderful job on her episode *Do No Harm*. Kelly continues, "I felt very anxious, but I trusted Damon's instincts and that he would know when we were ready. It was probably best that we waited because we had all this experience behind us and we really knew the show inside and out." Ragghianti continues, "So, we were called into the office and Damon and Carlton told us that we would definitely be getting a script the next year. That news really helped us stay focused and hungry and it just became a question of exactly when it was going to happen."

MATERNITY LEAVE

It was one of the most shocking and important episodes of season two, writers MATT RAGGHIANTI and DAWN LAMBERTSEN-KELLY discuss how *Maternity Leave* came to be, detailing the episode's early construct, the redrafts, right through to their reactions to their baby airing…

EMAILS

Matt Raggs
To: Dawn Kelly
December 18, 12:30am

Re: Uhh, this is taking a WHILE!!!

I fear I am obsessing about this, but would you please look over Act 3 and let me know if you feel I am on the right track?
Raggs

Dawn Kelly
To Matt Raggs
December 18, 2:31am

I'm probably obsessing, too. Here it is – 2:30 am! I could be wrong. Maybe it completely sucks. But it feels really good, Matt.

My first pass is attached. I'll read yours first thing in the morning and call you asap.
Dk

Matt Raggs
To: Dawn Kelly
December 19, 6:09pm

Re: Episode 215 complete

Here it is all the way through. Send me your final as soon as possible and then go have a beer. And then have another one; you did a GREAT job.
Raggs

Dawn Kelly
To Matt Raggs
December 19, 7:59 pm

Your half is great!
I'm jealous…

Hope they like it and we don't have too much to re-write. It's practically a script already!
Dk

"As we got further along in the [second] year, Dawn and I kept looking at each other going, 'I wonder when it's going to be?' he continues. "Damon then came in and told us it was probably going to be episode 13. We prepared ourselves for that and then at the last minute, we were told it wasn't going to be 13, but 15. So we knew exactly what script it was going to be for about a month, and then it was just a lot of sleepless nights getting there," he cracks. Kelly adds, "I had to pinch myself that it was finally happening! It doesn't seem real until you sit down and start typing."

While Dawn and Matt were also personal friends, they weren't an official writing team, as some writers are billed in Hollywood. Ragghianti explains, "We've written together, in so much that we write the diaries for the ABC website together, but that was really the extent of all the writing we've done as a team. We have helped each other with our other projects and specs, so I think we both had a pretty good idea of how the other person wrote and their style and mannerisms, but this is really the first time we've written a script together." Kelly adds, "I really respect his writing to begin with so if there was anyone I had to be paired with in this situation, it was great that it was him." Game about baring their creative souls to the world, the pair began to check in with *Lost Magazine* in December to document the details of not only the general writing process, but also their own personal exchanges as the writing evolved. Their odyssey officially began in early December of last year, as they broke the episode in the Writers' Room before Christmas break. The following is a diary of that journey:

PHONE INTERVIEW
DECEMBER 2005

Chatting about the initial scripting stages, Ragghianti shares, "It's such an interesting situation for us personally because of the fact that we are getting the 'Christmas script.' It's the script that takes place when everyone is out of the office [for the holiday break]. So we are not privy to the normal ins and outs of how these things are done. Normally, when you're on script, while the rest of the writing staff goes back into the Writers' Room to break the next episode, you and your partner stay in your office and work together there. But no one was around! But it's such a huge, huge step for Dawn and I. It can be the Christmas script, the 4th of July script – it doesn't make any difference to us – it's a script. We are thrilled. It's certainly not ideal working conditions, but I wouldn't trade it for the world and I know Dawn wouldn't either."

Splitting the episode between the two writers meant they had to first work out who wrote what. Kelly says, "It was a decision we made after talking to a bunch of the senior writers. All the scripts this season have been split and everyone does it a different way. Sometimes one person will write the flashbacks and then one person will write all the A-story." Ragghianti continues, "Obviously there are the growing pains and the process of feeling out who is right for each storyline and who was right for each act. It took us about 10 or 12 days to break the episode and I think we were both nervously wondering, 'Which part is she going to write and which part is he going to want to write?' In a stroke of luck, we both ended up getting to write the things we wanted to do. Dawn secretly wanted to write the teaser, acts one and two and thankfully, I wanted to write acts three, four and five."

On holiday as of the second week of December, Dawn and Matt were immediately charged with writing a detailed outline – a "break" – of the entire episode. They were responsible for their acts with the intention of merging them together to submit to Damon and Carlton before the end of the month. "We had such a good break, with most of the writers in the room with us," Kelly explains. "We all went over the break with a fine toothcomb and they made sure it was bullet proof – something that I think they did in order to protect us, making sure we had the best outline we could going into this. Walking out of there [after this discussion] and going into vacation, we knew the story backwards and forwards so it made it a lot easier. Ideally, you'd want to be in the office together because it is such a collaborative process, so you can write scenes and bounce it off the senior writers and get feedback right away. This has been awkward [writing it while being apart over the holiday season] because it is isolating and you're not sure if you are in the right direction. You are going off the outline, and it feels right, but it would be nice to have everyone around to get the immediate feedback."

PHONE INTERVIEW
DECEMBER 20, 2005

Slightly bleary from writing non-stop, Ragghianti details the situation, "Dawn and I have spent many, many hours on the phone over the course of the weekend and to make it even more interesting, Dawn left for her Christmas vacation. She's actually as we speak, somewhere in the jungles of Costa Rica. She had to call me collect last night. I got this operator over the line in Spanish asking if I would accept a collect call from Dawn and I said, "Si!" She emailed me her half and it's been absolutely crazy!" he laughs.

Adding her perspective in a later phone interview, Kelly adds, "I flew out on the 18th and drove to Tamarindo, which is six hours from the airport. There are dirt roads and we were really in the middle of nowhere. I was like, 'There is no way I am going to be able to get in touch with anyone!' My cell phone didn't work. The cell phone we rented didn't work. We got to the hotel and thank God, it had the only computer in the town. I was there every hour on the hour checking emails to get in touch with Matt. It makes me laugh that I was in the middle of nowhere doing this. It worked out though!"

Ragghianti continues, "So she sent me her half of the outline and I had mine as well. I sent both halves to Gregg Nations, who is our Script Coordinator. He compiled them together and put the scene numbers in there and sent it as a complete document to Damon and Carlton last night. I just got my notes from Carlton and I expect further notes from Damon later today. We'll talk on the phone to address the notes and address the further quotes and submit our finished outline to the network tomorrow. Carlton has given us the go-ahead to get started on the script. Before we left the office on Friday of last week, they let us know that we needed to have our first draft of the script ready on January 3 (2006)."

LOST

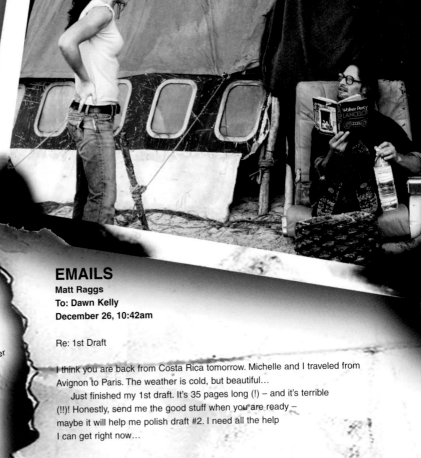

Proving even a vacation is never simple, Ragghianti details his script drama heading to France. "I'm on the plane to France. It's the first leg; we did it in legs, so we are flying from Los Angeles to Chicago. It's my very first episode of television. I'm sitting in First Class next to my wife thinking, 'What the hell happened to me?'" he laughs incredulously. "I have my outline there that we worked incredibly hard on from which we are writing the episode. I've got my laptop open, incredibly happy. I get up to go to the bathroom and I come back and as I am coming back down the aisle, my wife sees me and passes me for like the seventh time to use the bathroom on her own. As I'm walking back down, I look to my left and see that somebody's laptop is almost underwater. An entire cup of coffee has been spilled all over *my* laptop. My wife knocked over an entire cup of coffee on it. My outline is completely soaked. Thank God for David, the steward in First Class. I couldn't talk. He grabbed it out of my hands and starts wiping it down. I'm white as a sheet and he's saying, 'It's going to be okay.' I'll let it air out and I'm going to have your seat cleaned up.' Meanwhile, my wife comes out and sees me and asks, 'What's going on?' I said, 'Well, you just spilled a whole cup of coffee on my laptop.' She looks at me and says, 'But I was careful.' She is then of course almost in tears. Thank God, the laptop started… the most important thing I will write ever and it was underwater!"

EMAILS

Matt Raggs
To: Dawn Kelly
December 26, 10:42am

Re: 1st Draft

I think you are back from Costa Rica tomorrow. Michelle and I traveled from Avignon to Paris. The weather is cold, but beautiful…
Just finished my 1st draft. It's 35 pages long (!) – and it's terrible (!!)! Honestly, send me the good stuff when you are ready – maybe it will help me polish draft #2. I need all the help I can get right now…

Speak soon…

Welcome Home,
Raggs

Dawn Kelly
To: Matt Raggs
December 28, 11:37 am

Just got in late last night… flight delays and changes – hellish!
My plan is to stay home and write over the next seven days until this thing is due. I will send you a first draft as soon as I have something. Then we can give notes to each other and go back and forth with it until we get it right.
So feel free to send me what you have…
I'm sure it's a good start!
Dk

Dawn Kelly
To: Matt Raggs
December 30, 2:13 am

Re: Self-doubt has set in again….

I think your half is in GREAT SHAPE.
I love "parent trying to explain to their child for the 50th time why they need to brush their teeth."
You did a great job conveying the emotion all the way through. I made a couple of very small notes and edits… all minor stuff, which you can toss if you don't like.
Dk

EMAILS

Matt Raggs
To: Dawn Kelly
December 20, 4:38pm

Subject: Episode 215

Just got an email from CC [Carlton Cuse] with his revisions to the Outline. They are no big deal at all.

Hope your vacation is AWESOME. Because your outline IS!
Raggs

Matt Raggs
To: Dawn Kelly
December 21, 4:48pm

Re: Contact Numbers

I can't believe this is actually happening!!!

Hope you are having a great trip in Costa Rica and I look forward to reading an AMAZING draft from you as soon as it is ready. We know this story backwards and forwards, Dawn and I know the outline was a big success. We're gonna NAIL THIS! The only thing left to do now is get started.

See you in '06, baby!
Raggs

On December 24, Matt and his wife Michele travel to Paris, France to celebrate their one-year wedding anniversary with their parents.

Matt Raggs
To: Dawn Kelly
December 30, 11:35 am

Dude, it's going to be great. And I'm not saying that because I've spent the last three and a half hours sitting in a café drinking beer and writing. I really believe that. I've revised through the middle of Act 4...
Raggs

Matt Raggs
To: Dawn Kelly
December 31, 7:41 am

Re: Teaser 1 and 2 with my notes

I think you did a hell of a job DK – especially for the first draft. My notes throughout are minimal and... I am sending you the draft later this evening.

Happy, Happy, Happy NEW YEAR!
Raggs

PHONE INTERVIEW JANUARY 2, 2006

From her home in Los Angeles, Kelly updates the last week. "I've been back for a week, back at home writing in my office. When we were approved to go to script, that was when I took a breath and said, 'I'm OK now.' It was the third day into my trip and I put the computer away for a few days and enjoyed the trip because I knew when I got back I would have a week to just write. The hardest part for me was the outlining because I had never done that before. When I was writing features, I was doing index cards and scenes, but our outlines are so detailed. They are sometimes up to 25 pages. I think that we overwrote it because it was our first one and that was the big note we got. We turned in half a script! But going to script, I was excited. Once I got the outline done, I felt like that was the bulk of the work. The script was fun because then I could focus on dialogue. It was flowing well, but when I got to the end of the first script draft, I felt like I was just copying the outline. Then I went back to give it flavor and the emotion in everything, which is key. I talked to a couple of the writers over break, giving them pages and they said, 'Emotion, emotion, emotion.' Once you do that first pass, it's a skeleton, and then you go back and find the dialogue and the emotion. So, the first draft came pretty easily. The second and third were the ones I agonized over. Fortunately, we had the time to do that. In some cases, we had a disadvantage, but we had the advantage to be on break to have extra days to do this. It's been a blessing in disguise.

"So a lot of this week has been talking each other through things," she continues. "There is a lot of self-doubt that goes on and you second-guess yourself all the time, so it's been great to have each other to say, 'You're on the right track and this is working or not working.' Everyone as a writer has strengths and weaknesses that are coming out during this process. The fact that we can pick up slack for one another is important. *Lost* is such a big animal but having someone to bounce off of and help you is invaluable, especially as a new writer in TV. I've written features before and that is an isolated experience where you are off on your own. We are so fortunate to have this incredible group of writers to help us through this process. Damon and Carlton have been mentors to us in more ways than I can tell. I really feel that coming out of this, whatever happens, if I end up at *Lost* or somewhere else next season, I feel like I've been to the Ivy League. I know I can take this work experience and this writing training anywhere and feel really good about what I'm going to do.

"Matt is sending me his final draft tonight and I will put them together and send them to Gregg, who will take an editorial pass. From there it will go to Damon and Carlton. It will then go through another draft, then the network and then a production draft."

LOST

EMAILS

Matt Raggs
To: Dawn Kelly
January 2, 1:17pm

Re: Okay. Here we go…

Attached is my final draft of my half of the script. I'm sick to death of looking at this thing, but at the same time, I'm stoked for us both – because I know this is going to be an AMAZING episode and I can't believe we get to watch our names come on the screen under "Written By."

You did a HELL OF A JOB on your half, Dawn. And although I'm sure you're anxious and nervous and nauseous – just like I am – you should be confident in what you've done. It's really damn fine work.

See you in 24 hours…
Raggs

Dawn Kelly
To: Matt Raggs
January 2, 8:32pm

RE: Episode 215 Combined

Sorry that took so long… I read the whole thing through and it's singing! I'm so impressed with you, Matt. I think we can go in tomorrow with our heads high and wait to be re-written.
Dawn

Matt Raggs
To: Dawn Kelly
Jan. 3, 1:48 am

Awesome! I'll see you at the office and we'll read through together one more time. But I gotta tell you, I feel pretty darn good about the thing…
Raggs

E-MAILS
Dawn Kelly
To: Tara DiLullo
March 3, 2006

My dad flew in from New York. I was pretty nervous to begin with and through the whole thing my mind was racing… hoping everyone would be able to follow it despite the serialized nature of the show… hoping everyone would like the story. It was sort of painful.

When my name came up in the credits it was surreal… like it wasn't really happening, despite the loud cheering from our friends.

During the filming, we decided to watch the dailies, but to refrain from watching the final cut until it actually aired, hoping that would lend to the magic of the night. MISTAKE! I found myself incredibly distracted by things that had been cut for time.

Then when it was over, everyone was praising the episode, but I had no perspective on it. I took Thursday off to hang out with my Dad, so I didn't really get any feedback from the office and I wasn't checking e-mails, message boards or ratings.

So it wasn't until I went in on Friday that I learned it was a successful night. And it wasn't until watching it a second time this weekend (with my husband, who was out on his boat working Wednesday night) that it all really began to sink in and I was finally able to enjoy it.

Overall, I'm really proud of the work and the look on my Dad's face cancelled out all the uncomfortable moments. He so deserved to share the moment after supporting this crazy dream of mine for so long.

INTERVIEW AT DISNEY LOT, JANUARY 16, 2006

Two weeks later, Matt and Dawn sit down to lunch with me at the Disney Commissary to detail the script specifics of *Maternity Leave*. They are told that day the episode will run four minutes longer [than a normal episode's length], so they have to go back and add more material, which makes them both happy. Enthused about all the episode has to offer, Kelly details, "The theme is about Claire coming into motherhood. The story started with the concept of the flashback telling what happened to her already on the island when she was abducted. It put us in a different headspace because we knew we had plot we had to follow, whereas if you break a normal one you can come up with anything in someone's flashback." Ragghianti continues, "It's the first time we've done an island flashback ever. It's really exciting. It was a completely new paradigm for the show and an exciting prospect for us to do it like that. In this episode, we had two things to deal with with Claire. One is the fact that we know a little bit about her. We knew she was going to give up the baby, but not exactly why. Now you have someone thrust into a situation where in the best of circumstances you're not ready for it. Everybody who thinks they might be ready to have a kid never is, and that dynamic is exacerbated to the nth degree being on an island where you don't have access to doctors and medical things. She's in a panic. What do you do if something goes wrong with your child when you are on a deserted island? Granted, you have a doctor and a hatch with a washing machine, but you are going to freak out, and that's what happens here. In the course of freaking out, something is triggered in Claire's memory and we get to learn a little bit more about what happened to her in those 10 days where she was missing on the island. We get to find out where she was and what happened to her. It was difficult because there were no rules to follow, but exciting for the same reason. We got to make it up. Everybody is interested in what happened to her and where she was. We got to go down that path and the surprises are creepy."

Asked about cuts that needed to be made to the script during the revision process, Kelly says there were some. "Sure, there is stuff you get attached to and you don't want to give up. The outline was very wordy because we wanted to be super-descriptive and make sure everything was in there. It hurts a little to give those things up. Eddie (Kitsis) and Adam (Horowitz) came in and were assigned to guide us through the notes process because we obviously have never done this before. They have done this 10 times now with Damon, so they were able to interpret the notes and say, 'We don't need this' or what they meant by this to get through that. They were a fresh pair of eyes that helped us and made it a lot better. It makes the scenes pop more and read easier. At the end of the day, yeah, you don't want to give stuff up, but it's for the best of the script." Ragghianti concurs saying, "It worked out great. People would ask us how the notes process went and we didn't have anything to compare it to." Kelly chimes in, "We thought it was a breeze and painless…" Ragghianti laughs adding, "But for all we know it could have been the worst note session of all time, in television history, but it seemed like it went great."

With the script now relatively complete, the pair quickly relate their favorite parts from each other's sections. Ragghianti offers of Dawn's work, "There are a couple of them. The first real flashback on the island takes place during an OB exam for Claire. It's extraordinary and is just the creepiest thing you'd ever want to see. It's really well done. The flashbacks are always more fun because they are so much richer and you can get outside of the island world, so it's a bit of a cheat for me to say, but the second flashback was put in last minute and it's so good. They are both superb." Kelly laughs and says, "Poor Matt got stuck with the female script. It's all about women. But the first flashback in Act Three is incredible. Matt is a very eloquent writer. He brought it home and it was so emotional that I almost had tears in my eyes the way he wrote it and I knew the story. I knew what was going to happen and he tied it all together and hit the grand slam. So the penultimate scene of his is my favorite." Ragghianti cracks with a smile, "Under this mustache, I've got a soft side."

Maternity Leave aired on March 1, 2006. After four months and countless lessons learned, Matt and Dawn share how they watched the episode together in a hotel room in Manhattan Beach, California with their friends and family on that milestone Wednesday night…

PHONE INTERVIEW APRIL 20, 2006

Ragghianti offers his perspective, sharing, "Dawn was fantastic and arranged the whole thing and there was wine and pizza and beer. My wife and me, my best friend Dave and his fiancée and a couple of other very close friends were there. I'd say there were about 20 of us in that hotel room. It was as utterly nerve-wracking as anything that has ever happened to me in my life. Honestly, I thought it was going to be this extraordinary swell of emotion. I can't express to you how uncomfortable it was start to finish. I know the reason now, in hindsight, was that neither of us watched the early cuts because we wanted to maintain this special moment. As a consequence, we weren't prepared for the little bits that got cut. In fact, one whole scene of mine was moved from act four to act five, so all I could do through the entire episode was worry about what had been cut. I almost felt like I was worried more about what the episode wasn't than what it was. But the instant the episode ended, I felt fantastic and had a great time, but the lesson was learned – watch the early cuts!" he laughs. "It was so uncomfortable and I thought it was just me, but I went back to the office the next day and every writer said, 'Nope, that's really what it's like!' Every writer is neurotic enough to sweat it out and this was with 20 million people watching!" Reflecting on what he did like, Ragghianti says, "I was really pleased with the scene where Ethan and Claire are sitting on the log and she is very childlike. He is very supportive and protective and tells her that he is going to miss her. When I wrote it, I had a very clear image in my mind of what I wanted it to look like and it was almost exactly taken from my mind's eye. I was really struck that it was exactly how I imagined it." With a sigh and smile in his voice, Raggs finishes by offering, "Overall, I'm thrilled that it came off the way that it did."

SEE YOU ON THE OTHER SIDE

The Others. They are all here: the faux bearded Mr. Friendly, played by **M.C. GAINEY**; the actor behind master-of-stealth Goodwin, **BRETT CULLEN**; Ethan Rom's off-screen persona **WILLIAM MAPOTHER**; the mysterious teenager Alex, played by **TANIA RAYMONDE**; the Other with a penchant for blood, Pickett, brought to life by **MICHAEL BOWEN**; actress **APRIL GRACE** analyzes her zen-like Ms. Klugh; and last – but by no means least – **MICHAEL EMERSON** discusses his terrifying portrayal of Henry Gale...

"With the finale, I read the script and I had goose bumps. It was bizarre and amazing. I was so intrigued by that sound. What the heck is it?"
— April Grace (Ms. Klugh)

"People asked me all summer, 'Why did you kidnap the boy?' My response was that I saw it as an at-sea rescue."
— M.C. Gainey (Mr. Friendly)

Who

are the Others?! It's the confounding question that has become one of *the* greatest enigmas of *Lost,* which is no small feat considering the abundance of other puzzling threads yet to be explained on the show. Hinted at by Danielle Rousseau and then scarily personified by the deranged Ethan during season one, the Others became the proverbial boogeymen, hovering in the background of the action until *Exodus (Part Two)*. In that finale, the harrowing kidnapping of Walt at sea by a gnarly band of people on a boat proved once and for all the existence of the Others and that they weren't looking to help anyone get home safely. In one fell swoop, they took Walt, shot Sawyer and set fire to the raft, instigating a whole new nightmare for the survivors of Flight 815.

A huge piece of *Lost's* sophomore season focused on revealing more details about the Others. Their stronghold on the island is now known to be deep and with the revelation of subtle clues and truths, it's even clearer that they are not at all what anyone expected. With cunning tactics (Goodwin), fake beards and costumes, and even elaborate sets, the Others are playing on the weaknesses of the survivors with precision for an end that is far from being ultimately revealed. For the small repertoire of actors cast to play the Others over the last two seasons, the mysteries are no less compelling or even understood. One and all, the actors all admit to being in the dark about who their characters are individually or as part of the larger group, yet that they are all relishing the opportunity to add their pieces to a story they (and we) can't wait to discover. *Lost Magazine* recently gathered all of the Others together to talk exclusively about what they think about their characters and what's yet to be discovered about their creepy modus operandi…

As the man behind the wheel in *Exodus (Part Two)*, Mr. Friendly became the angry, aggressive, bearded follow-up to Ethan's lead in portraying the Others. But you'll find none of those qualities in M.C. Gainey, the gregarious, funny actor behind the fake beard. Having already worked with *Lost* Executive Producer Carlton Cuse a few years ago on *The Adventures of Brisco County Jr.,* Gainey says he got a new call from Cuse last year to join them in Hawaii for the season finale. "The unique thing about it was that I had no clue who the character was, or what he was going to do and I just took it on faith," the actor says. "When they said it was going to be interesting, I said, 'OK!' When I got there I had no idea why I was kidnapping Walt. I had no idea what or who I was. It was one of the most interesting acting experiences I've ever had, because all the things we usually build a character on, the character history and what he wants, I knew none of that!" But Gainey says he created his own answers to those questions in the summer between seasons. "People asked me all summer, 'Why did you kidnap the boy?' My response was that I saw it as an at-sea rescue. I saw an unprotected youth on a burning raft, with no adults in sight, so I rescued him. The fact that I shot those people and set that raft on fire, notwithstanding. I tried to put a positive spin on that and who knows, it might be right!" he laughs deeply.

This season, Gainey returned for five episodes where we saw his character evolve from the mysterious heavy to an almost sheepish guy literally playing his part with his fellow Others. As audiences followed that

evolution, so too did the actor. "When we did the campfire scene [in *The Hunting Party*], I had no idea that I was wearing a costume – that it would be revealed that I was actually wearing a costume and a fake beard!" Gainey admits. "I was playing it like it was my real beard and I was a barefooted guy. As we now know, it wasn't a real beard and I think that we'll be wearing shoes the next time you see us," he smiles.

As to his own theories about his character, Gainey offers, "My thoughts were that whatever the mission was, whatever we were about, we were much better organized than we appeared to be. We appeared to be villains, but I'm not sure that we are. I try to keep a sense of role-playing going. For instance, in the campfire scene, trying to disarm them can be interpreted in two different ways, one to make it easier for me to kill them, or to disarm them so they don't kill us. Basically, I don't have a take on what we are about. I am prepared to boil them in a pit and eat them, or enlighten them to a higher state of consciousness. There's no way to know," he laughs. "But the one thing I am trying to do with Mr. Friendly is to try to bring a little levity to it. Henry Gale? Have we seen him smile or laugh once? With Mr. Friendly, I'm trying to lighten it up a little bit with him. He seems like a folksy kind of guy, but that may not be true either!" Only next season will tell and Gainey hopes to be back to tell the full Others' story. "I just assumed it was a one-time job. I was delighted to go back this year and I'm even more delighted to go back next year."

In *The Other 48 Days*, the Others took a front seat in the story alongside the introduction of the Tailies. The tension-filled arc that found Ana Lucia staging a battle of

"I don't know if she is completely innocent, but for the moment she is sympathetic [towards Claire] ... I'm curious to see what happens with that whole angle."
— Tania Raymonde (Alex)

wits against Goodwin until he finally revealed his Other nature was a suspenseful highlight of the season and a thrill for the actor behind Goodwin, Brett Cullen. The busy actor was called in to read for the part last year and he recalls simply, "I went in and read for them and they offered me the part and I said, 'Let's go!'" Unlike the other actors, Cullen's character got his beginning, middle and end in the one episode, but he admits a lot still changed from script to screen. "You take it for face value what they write in the script, but there are certain nuances in the script that sometimes don't make it to the cut. There was a flirtation with Michelle's character, Ana Lucia, and mine that didn't really play out in the shooting. My concept, and what I was trying to play, was that I had sort of chosen her as my mating partner. One – she was the powerhouse of the tail section and that I wanted to make sure I had a handle on that and one way of doing it was romantically. Two – you don't really know where the Others are coming from or what their agenda is, other than that they are perceived as evil or bad because they've taken the children. So he does flirt with her and some of that was cut out, but some of it played. I don't know how much was supposed to be visualized, but that's how I saw it."

Asked his favorite moment of the episode, Cullen quickly offers, "It was the scene with Michelle where we finally sit down and have that discussion, when she says, "You weren't in the jungle. You weren't even wet." You see the expression on my face… the Camera Operator, Paul Edwards, who I've worked with a couple of times, called me after and said, 'It was very subtle, just the crick of your neck, but then you knew.'" I kept thinking after that, you see me sit up, where his backbone gets rigid and he goes, 'Let's tussle.' I was kind of inspired by Ben Kingsley's character in *Sexy Beast*."

Cullen continues, "Carlton called me after the show aired and he said, 'I don't call guest stars very often, but you were so fantastic and really realized the character and I'm really pissed off we killed you. Listen, no one dies on *Lost* so don't be surprised if we call you again.' They did call me for *Maternity Leave*, but I was working and they were rewriting and then figured out it wouldn't make such sense to do it." Laughing, he adds, "I was going to call Carlton and

say, 'I have a better idea! Why don't you have Goodwin's twin brother, who is actually the leader of the Others be Badwin… Goodwin and Badwin.'" The actor says he hopes the next season will allow his character to come back in some flashbacks, so he can continue the fun. "It's a different, dramatic series that, to me, merits attention. As an actor it's a great opportunity. As a surfer, it's an even better opportunity because they shoot it in Hawaii!"

At the halfway point of the season, *Maternity Leave* gave a us a glimpse of two more Others of note that figured heavily into the brief history of the series. First off, Ethan, the first Other to show his face returned in Claire's flashback, which filled in the blanks of what happened to her while she was kidnapped. William Mapother, who gave a stunningly sinister performance in season one. The actor was thrilled to return, albeit briefly, and remembers how challenging those first appearances on the show were. "I had no idea what it was going to be like. I asked the writers and producers all sorts of questions about the character. The first couple scripts certainly didn't answer any of the questions so I said, 'Guys. How do you want me to do it?' Their answer was to have me shoot almost every shot six or seven ways: angry, loving, scary, frightened, crazy, mechanical! It was like an acting exercise. So before my episodes came on, I had no idea what he was going to be like. I still have a lot of questions about the character, but I know a little bit more now," he smiles.

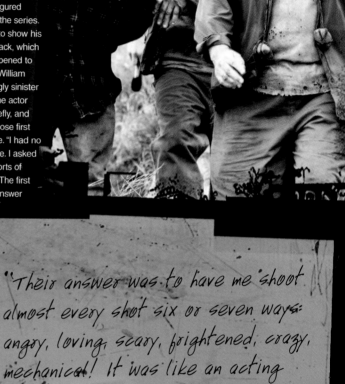

> "Their answer was to have me shoot almost every shot six or seven ways: angry, loving, scary, frightened, crazy, mechanical! It was like an acting exercise."
> — William Mapother (Ethan)

Also in those flashbacks, we get to glimpse a young woman that looks remarkably like fellow island castaway, Danielle Rousseau (Mira Furlan), who in turn is looking for her long lost child, Alex. For actress Tania Raymonde, that connection to the character is a surprising outcome that wasn't part of her initial casting. "In the beginning, the name of the character when they cast me was Jessica," the actress reveals. "There was no mention of Danielle Rousseau. I was cast under the assumption that I would play a girl named Jessica and then I guess things evolved from there. In the first episode, there was no name change and they referred to me as a young girl. At the end of *Maternity Leave*, Danielle mentions something to Claire and Claire says there was a girl that saved her and Danielle reacts like she has found her daughter. At the end of

"I was going to call Carlton [Cuse – Executive Producer] and say, 'I have a better idea! Why don't you have Goodwin's twin brother, who is actually the leader of the Others be Badwin.... Goodwin and Badwin.'"
— Brett Cullen (Goodwin)

Three Minutes they refer to me as Alex directly and that's when I took on that name. There was no indication as to what was going to happen."

Like her fellow Others, Raymonde is unsure of exactly what Alex's real intentions are. While Alex helped Claire escape the medical hatch, that still doesn't explain why. "What was difficult was not knowing exactly what her goal was – not knowing the path of the character or if she knew anything about Claire in the past," the actress offers. "No questions

were answered, so you just go with it and trust the script in front of you. I don't know if she is completely innocent, but for the moment she is sympathetic [towards Claire]. I'm curious to see what happens with that whole angle."

In the last third of the season, Michael's return to the hatch sparks the revelation of a whole new set of Others, those operating in a camp where Walt was being held. Headed by a regal, authoritative woman who calls herself Ms. Klugh, she works with a man

named Pickett to draw blood from Michael and she then interrogates Michael about his son and his fellow survivors. Veteran character actor Michael Bowen plays the toadie with the syringe and he admits his previous body of work playing dark characters got him the gig. "They knew my work and that's how they called me. Carlton Cuse said, 'I want you to be Bowen. Be funny and scary.' I said, 'I can do that!'" he laughs.

It turns out that had to be enough because the actor admits he didn't get much more direction than

"I'm going to be back in season three and one of the places the show is going to go is 'Other-ville.' We are going to take our hostages back to the base from which we operate and that base may be a surprising change of scene for the audience." — Michael Emerson

that. "I had to make things up because they can't tell you. They have a policy – they don't tell you what's happening. I still don't know what we are or what is going on, even after watching the finale! But just from the action I had to do, when I take blood from Michael's arm, it all looks like I know what I'm doing. I had to create some sort of a reality there. I looked at all the plane crash survivors as though I was a psychologist observing them. I had to come up with something and that was my choice and how I approached it. I don't know if they are evil. I'm wondering if they are in some type of experiment. Maybe they were told they were in a plane crash and maybe they have been there for many, many years and this is the way they evolved or devolved? I don't know it's hard to say. It can go anywhere. There was a great series, *The Prisoner*, that had the same type of feeling and it was brilliant. I think the public has matured enough and are becoming more educated and these type of shows sell and that's great."

While his motivation may be hazy, Bowen says the actual experience of working with the cast was nothing but a pleasure. "I've worked with M.C. a few times and I love him. Everyday going to work with him makes life fun and easy. What I notice is that when you are working with great actors, you can't begin to understand how much easier it is. When I got to the set, I noticed how efficient the whole system was. It felt professional and therefore relaxing. Everyone had been there for two years and they are down in the dirt and they're not complaining. It was impressive. It's why it comes out the way it does."

For April Grace, Ms. Klugh (a.k.a. Bea), her part in the show came about like many of her fellow cast – with a simple call. "I got a call from Damon [Lindelof] first, he told me what was happening on the show with the Others. Then I got my script and was told to just do your thing – without a net," she laughs. "I was able to just make up whatever back-story I wanted. It was really exciting."

"I decided that the Others aren't bad," she continues. "It's all about understanding perception and I thought they were there first and what if something literally started living on your land? What would you do? You'd say, 'They're not going to occupy us!' Also, given the information I have, I have to believe we're doing something good. In my head, I was thinking maybe she was a nun, which gave me the possibilities of playing her as righteous, spiritual and stereotypically stern. It was fun to think of that, plus there was nothing else to go on!"

In three episodes at the end of the season, Grace shares, "I had a wonderful time. There were fires burning and the sets looked so authentic; all I had to do was look at Harold [Perrineau] and go for it. I was obviously in a position of power, as he was tied up and so it was wonderful being assertive with an adversary."

The actress says she was pleased to end the season on such a high note. "With the finale, I read the script and I had goose bumps. It was bizarre and amazing. I was so intrigued by that sound. What the heck is it? And when we shot that scene, the island is 'shaking' – we are all moving around pretending it is – and there were a couple of moments of levity in there because we just looked at one another doing that and you are just feeling ridiculous," she laughs. Confirming her recurring status next season, Grace smiles, "I'm grateful for whatever time I get on the show!"

Of course, you can't even discuss the Others without mentioning the one man that electrified the screen for the last half of the season – Henry Gale. Posing as another shipwrecked play toy of fate, Gale was beaten, harassed, cajoled and even reasoned with to reveal his true identity as an Other and yet he never cracked. In fact,

he played the survivors like psychological labs rats in his game of manipulating that was mesmerizing to watch. Thanks to the talents of actor Michael Emerson, Gale defined the potential of the Others and set the stage for season three. Musing about h character, Emerson offers, "I've never been sure he is a villain and I think the audience fears or worries about him a little bit because his agenda is unknow to them. In the finale, when he says that they are t good guys, maybe he is in some way, and it makes me think my instincts were right. When people ask me what is the essence of Henry Gale, I said, 'He behaves like a commando behind enemy lines.' It doesn't mean he is a bad guy. It just means his mission is a sensitive one and dangerous… and it clearly been all of that," he chuckles evilly.

Revealing his part in season three, Emerson teases, "In season three, one of the places the s is going to go is 'Other-ville.' We are going to tak our hostages back to the base from which we operate and that base may be a surprising change of scene for the audience. All I know is that they destroyed all the sets they have on the soundstages [in Hawaii] and they are building some really strange and interesting n environments. I think it's fair to say that the Ot that we have come to know – that ragtag Robinson's Crusoe army – that's not a how they are. They have other looks other places to go. It's still a comple mystery to me. I talked to Carlton C and Damon Lindelof last week and said, 'We have great things in min They asked if I had anything to ta about and I said, 'No, I love going wherever you guys send me.' The said, 'Hang on, because we are to have some interesting stuff…

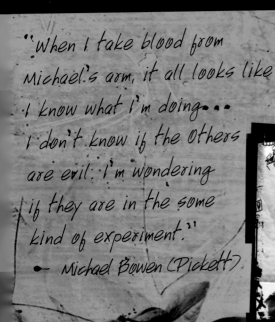

"When I take blood from Michael's arm, it all looks like I know what I'm doing... I don't know if the Others are evil. I'm wondering if they are in the some kind of experiment."
— Michael Bowen (Pickett)

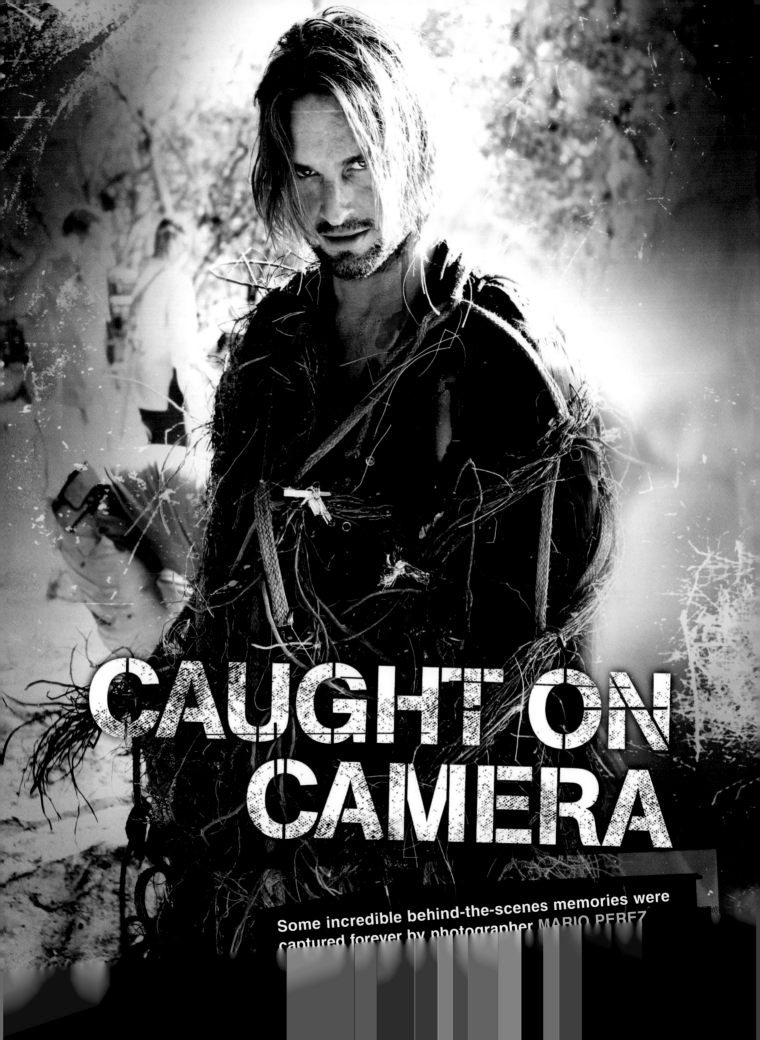

CAUGHT ON CAMERA

Some incredible behind-the-scenes memories were
captured forever by photographer MARIO PEREZ

That paper cup doesn't look like a Dharma coffee to me... Terry O'Quinn (Locke) relaxes between takes

Team *Lost* prepare to shoot a sequence inside The Hatch set...

pages.

Ce passeport cont

CARRIER:
OCE

NAME:
JAC

FROM:
S

FLIGHT
8

BOAR

SEA

23

Head of Make-up Steve LaPorte adds some final touches to William Mapother (Ethan)...

Daniel Dae Kim (Jin) prepares for one of the early flashback sequences of season two's fifth episode... *And Found*

The incredible feat of creating a scene set in Iraq but filmed in Hawaii is almost complete...

It's all about the steadicam when shooting the Nigerian drug plane's 'cremation' sequence in *The 23rd Psalm*...

Sleeping with the enemy – it's time for Brett Cullen's (Goodwin) close-up during the Tail section survivors' first night on the island...

Evangeline Lilly (Kate) and James Horan (Wayne Jansen) during a break from filming the revelatory flashback scenes from the second season's ninth epsiode *What Kate Did*...

The paint job on any set always adds that final touch of detail and realism...

LOST

Naveen Andrews (Sayid) chills out on the tarmac between flashback shots for *One of Them*, set in Iraq...

Matt Earl Beesley directs Adewale Akinnuoye-Agbaje (Mr. Eko) during *The 23rd Psalm*'s poignant moment where Eko finds the dead body of his brother...

Some light relief – Matthew Fox (Jack), Michelle Rodriguez (Ana Lucia), Evangeline Lilly (Kate), Josh Holloway (Sawyer), and Terry O'Quinn (Locke) share a joke together on the beach

This fantastic photograph shows you the amount of work and set-up that goes into even the most basic of *Lost* shots...

Our merry band of heroes Naveen Andrews (Sayid), Michelle Rodriguez (Ana Lucia) and Dominic Monaghan (Charlie)

DEAR DIARY

"The sand is deep and when you go for a walk on the beach here, it's a serious workout..."

"My wife and I found a house that has a stunning view of the North Shore. I go down and walk on the beach just to stay in shape. The sand is deep and when you go for a walk on the beach here, it's a serious workout. You don't do it for very long. Another thing, a lot of fans come up, but they don't come up in droves. They come up – one or two. They are on vacation, happy and tanned and glad to see a member of LOST. It's such a delight. I just love talking to those people and spending time with them. For example, yesterday, I'm walking past the pipeline on the North Shore and the waves were perfect. There are 100 guys out there riding 20 foot waves and just behind the guys are whales breeching and I thought, 'There is no where else on Earth where you can see this.' And then a woman next to me says, 'Oh my!' I turned around and she says to me, 'We are watching these guys surf... and then there are whales breeching... and then John Locke comes walking by! This is the coolest place!' It's pretty cool for me too.'"

"I THINK WE FOUND IT..."

Take a deep breath and get ready to relive the season two finale, complete with exclusive photography and extracts from the shooting script...

115   INT. MONITORING STATION - NIGHT

A WINDOW. FROSTED OVER.
AND it's SNOWING OUTSIDE. We're
          someplace really COLD!
WE PAN OFF the window to --

MATHIAS. BUNDLED IN A PARKA. Thirty.
                Hip. Techie. He
KICKS a FRITZING SPACE HEATER.

        MUTTERS under his breath as --

          HENRIK (O.S.)
Don't bother. It's busted...

He makes his way through a RACKS OF
          TOWERS AND A MAZE OF
      COMPUTER GEAR over to his buddy --

HENRIK, late 30s, bearded and equally
techo-geeky, who is
     hunched over a CHESS BOARD.
          He also wears a RATTY PARKA --
gloves missing the fingertips.
          Moves his BISHOP, SMILES --

                    HENRIK (CONT'D)
          I crush your Najdorf Sicilian
          defense -- and that is the last you
          shall see of your rook.

Ah. But that wasn't ENGLISH.
In fact... it's a language we
          can't quite put our finger on.
PORTUGUESE? FINNISH? NATIVE
AMERICAN? And unfortunately?

          NO SUBTITLES.

                    MATHIAS
          All part of the plan, my friend.
                    HENRIK
          Ah. Then your plan must be to
          lose. Please. Your move.

But Mathias? Ain't moving anything.

                    He's in SHOCK.

                         HENRIK (CONT'D)
          What?

Matthias POINTS over Henrik'S SHOULDER. His voice QUAKES --

                    MATHIAS
          How long has it been doing that?

Henrik follows Mathias's gaze to a MONITOR tucked a midst a
bunch of other monitors and computer gear. On a BLACK BOX
TAPED to the TOP OF THE MONITOR (and wired to the back) a RED
LIGHT IS BLINKING. Henrik furrows his brow, CONCERNED --

He looks closer at the monitor. A NUMBER appears there all
alone on the SCREEN: 7418880.

>/ 7418880
Electromagnetic
Anomaly
Detected

Matthias looks PANICKED.   Henrik GRABS A BINDER and
FLIPS RAPIDLY THROUGH THE PAGES.   Mathias can barely wait --

            MATHIAS (CONT'D)
That's _it_, isn't it? We   HENRIK
missed it again, didn't -- ?   -- _We didn't miss it!_

        Whatever Henrik finds in the binder is CONFIRMATION.
And that's when the SOUNDS start. BEEP. WHIR. BEEP.

And now our GUYS ARE IN PANIC MODE. They both LEAP UP,
Mathias accidentally bonks the table -- UPENDING the CHESS
BOARD -- pieces SCATTERING EVERYWHERE as --

            MATHIAS (CONT'D)
Oh, so this time you're _not_ going
to claim it's a _false alarm_? An
erroneous _error message_ -- ?

Henrik is typing like crazy on
another KEYPAD across the room

            HENRIK
-- Just _shut up_ and call while I
        send the telex, Mathias!

A beat. Mathias shakes his head...
then reaches for a CHIPPED
BRIGHT YELLOW PHONE. Picks it up.

There's no DIAL TONE.

But he looks right at his EXCITED
partner as he calmly speaks
into the phone in ENGLISH --

Afterword

Greetings Dharma farmers,

When Titan Books told me that they were planning to create this 'Best of' collection from Lost Magazine so far, I thought, "Fantastic!" which was almost immediately followed by, "How many pages can it be...?" Simply because — thanks to the ongoing incredible time, support and input that the entire Lost Team put into every single issue — we have clocked up a huge amount of fascinating material so far. Just like the official magazine for Alias some years ago now, editing Lost Magazine since its launch has been an absolute pleasure — and this collection of hand-picked articles circa season two will hopefully reflect why.

The cast and crew have always been extremely generous with their time, ideas — and often with their own, personal photographs — of their experiences on Lost, and this is something which has always made each edition different and special in its own unique way. At the time of writing this afterword, I've just seen the incredible eighth episode of the fifth season — how time flies, huh? Which is why revisiting all of the exclusive interviews and behind-the-scenes features we put together for season two (the first six issues of the magazine) has been a really enjoyable nostalgic trip and a great reminder of our first introduction to the Dharma Initiative...

Special thanks to Damon Lindelof, Carlton Cuse, J.J. Abrams, Noreen O'Toole, Samantha Thomas, Adam Horowitz, Eddy Kitsis, Melissa Harling and all at Team Lost, ABC and Bad Robot for always giving so much of your time and energy to this magazine: we literally couldn't do it without you.

Hope to see you in the future for another 'Best Of' collection...

Namaste,

Paul Terry
Editor
Lost: The Official Magazine